ADVANCED SALMON FISHING

Lessons from Experience

ADVANCED SALMON FISHING

Lessons from Experience

Neil Graesser

THE BOYDELL PRESS

First published 1987 by The Boydell Press
an imprint of Boydell & Brewer Ltd
PO Box 9, Woodbridge, Suffolk IP12 3DF
and Wolfeboro, New Hampshire 03894-2069, USA

ISBN 0 85115 464 6

British Library Cataloguing in Publication Data

Graesser, Neil
    Advanced salmon fishing.
    1. Salmon fishing
    I. Title
    799.1'755   SH684

    ISBN 0–85115–464–6

Library of Congress Cataloging in Publication Data

Graesser, Neil.
    Advanced salmon fishing.

    1. Salmon-fishing. I. Title.
SH684.G727 1987   799.1'755   87–735
ISBN 0–85115–464–6 (U.S.)

Printed in Great Britain by
St Edmundsbury Press, Bury St Edmunds, Suffolk

CONTENTS

An Angler's Chance of Success

No-one who reads this book could be blamed for thinking that the whole thing is a bit far-fetched. Nearly every story tells of many fish being caught and I hardly ever mention the countless hours and days that I have spent flogging the water in fruitless search for a taking fish. I apologise for this, but I would like to put the book in the right perspective. In these stories I hope to illustrate certain important points about fishing and catching fish. It is therefore important to give illustrations of success that can be attributed to one cause or another. After all, if I related a story about any one of my countless blank days it would just tell you that I had a blank day – nothing else. These red letter incidents have come to me over nearly fifty years fishing experience, and during several of these years I was lucky enough to fish on fine beats of good salmon rivers some time every day for at least five days a week throughout the entire fishing season.

Having said that, I think that the first thing to do if you are to become a successful fisherman is to study the salmon itself. As we all know salmon are born in fresh water and spend the first one to three years as fry or parr feeding in fresh water. They then migrate to the sea as smolts when they are between four inches and six inches in length and weighing a mere two to three ounces. Once they migrate to the sea they feed voraciously on many other types of small fish and crustacea, supplementing their diet with plankton. They establish a quite extraordinary growth rate and weight gain during this period of their life at sea. When they return to fresh water after spending one sea winter at sea as grilse they weigh on average five to six pounds, and if they spend two sea winters or more at sea they then return as salmon averaging ten pounds in weight, some fish being very much heavier. Their sole purpose when they return to fresh water is to regenerate the species. At this stage of their life cycle nature equips them with the ability to survive a complete fast regardless of how long they spend in fresh water before spawning. They do not have to feed daily to sustain themselves as do other freshwater fish. Obviously therefore their taking habits are absolutely unpredictable and this does not make the salmon fisherman's task of catching them easier.

Although an angler can be casting over salmon throughout the entire day, because they are not forced to eat he may well not get a single offer. What he has got to find is a salmon that is in a taking mood or a salmon that can be fooled or bamboozled into taking his lure or bait by the wiles or persistence of the fisherman himself.

The other very important factor in salmon fishing is knowledge of your water. This applies more to fly fishing and fishing on spate rivers which are subject to continual fluctuations in water levels. Fish change their lies in a pool according to the water flow and even a two inch rise or fall in water level can make a vast difference to the position of the best taking places. And this can apply throughout the entire beat of a river. It doesn't really matter if the angler possesses this knowledge himself or is accompanied by a ghillie, who knows the water well. In either case the angler will be able to concentrate his efforts entirely on the more productive areas of his beat, and this alone is a huge advantage because it saves him from wasting a considerable amount of his precious time fishing water where his chances would be slim or non-existent.

Most good taking lies are incredibly consistent not only throughout the season but also from year to year, unless they are destroyed when the bed of the river is altered as a result of a severe spate. The main lies of a beat can often be responsible between them for producing a significant percentage of the annual catch of that beat. Many of them are sited across varying widths of the river or anywhere throughout the entire length of a pool. Some of them may be clearly read by the experienced angler because of some tell-tale swirl or blemish on the surface denoting an underwater object, while others are completely disguised. It is these lies that a stranger to the beat can miss consistently either because he does not cast far enough across the river or because he does not work his fly close enough into the bank. On other occasions a newcomer to a beat might not start high enough up the pool or even stop fishing too soon. There is very often a lie right at the tail of a pool particularly if there is a long stretch of rough water below it. Missing these vital lies can mean the difference between success or failure and can make a significant difference to the number of fish caught. Sometimes an angler new to a beat may be lucky and cover all the lies by chance. But this is unlikely and I doubt whether anyone, however fine a fisherman, will ever take anything like the full potential out of a new beat without guidance. However, provided the angler has a good memory and is observant he will soon gain this vital knowledge for himself through experience as he gets to know his beat better.

Many anglers fail to realise how little actual taking water there may be in a huge expanse of river. This will vary with the height of the river and it also varies from pool to pool due mainly to the river bed formation. Also pools and taking places change considerably with the differing seasons of the year. Early in the spring the rocky pools or deep dead pools have their heyday, in the summer again rocky pools, shallow fast flowing runs and canal-like stretches can all provide good sport, whilst in the autumn the plainer gravelly pools and shallower areas of the river often gain precedence over the deeper rocky water. Knowledge of the river or information gleaned from a ghillie or local fisherman can easily, during all seasons of the year, be the keystone to success.

Another aspect of salmon fishing can probably best be summed up by the double question: what beat? when? If you want to catch fish, then you have to take a beat for one week, one fortnight, or one month during the year. Only the very luckiest will fish more. Twenty or thirty years ago the prime time to go salmon fishing was in the spring and the best beats were usually located in the lower and central sections of the river system. Now this has somewhat changed. First of all the traditional spring run has declined and secondly, since the advent of UDN disease, the number of kelts that survive spawning and inhabit the lower sections of the rivers as they drop down to the sea in the early months of the year has shown a drastic decline. Because salmon are gregarious creatures, early fish used to enter the river system and they often occupied pools inhabited by kelts. Now, as the kelts are fewer, the spring salmon are more inclined to push higher up our river systems in search of company when they first enter a river. This inclination to push further up a river system can be accentuated by warmer water temperatures, particularly after a mild winter. Often nowadays the best time to fish the lower reaches of a big river like the Tay or Tweed is in the autumn when the autumn run of fish comes in.

The central beats of a river can be good for most of the year, although in some cases you will find even the summer runs of fish going straight through these beats. This does depend of course from river to river. Upper beats of any river usually start slowly but then they will catch fish later in the year, and as the season progresses they may be the most productive on the river. Rivers which have falls or high weirs can be exceptions to this general pattern because each formidable fall or weir has its own water temperature control. These vary from 38°F–52°F according to the size and height of the barrier and fish will not ascend these obstructions until the water temperature in the river reaches the right level. If, therefore, there is a formidable barrier low down on the river, as on the Cassley, fish will be held below it until April or May when the water temperature reaches 52°F.

All this, in practice, is largely theoretical. What is not theoretical is the actual likelihood of catching a fish when you are there casting on the river bank. It is a fact that salmon are more easily caught when they have just settled in a lie in a pool. If they have been in the same lie in the same pool for several days, they become stale and are then much more difficult to catch. And it is not until they move on upstream or are moved out of their lie by a spate that they really become catchable again. Fish can also be caught if they happen to rest for a while in a run or small pool or, indeed, in any other type of pool as they ascend the river system. The tail of a pool just above long rapids or some distance upstream from the next pool downstream, is a favourite place to find and catch resting fish particularly in high water flows. Fish from the summer runs who move upstream when the water temperature is over 50°F can travel very long distances without resting, and it is these fish that are extremely difficult (if not impossible) to catch unless they happen to rest somewhere in the beat that the angler is fishing. I am sure that all experienced anglers will agree that it is most frustrating to fish all day fruitlessly, with fish moving in every pool that refuse to take any notice of anything that is presented to them. But this is typical of the behaviour of either running or stale fish and the angler has just got to fish on and on in the hope that he will come across the fool in the family.

The most important factor in salmon fishing, certainly for fly fishing, is the air to be warmer than the water. This is more important than water levels or any weather condition you can think of. If you have a 5°–10°F difference between the air and water temperatures (with the former being higher) this is ideal, and this is one of the main reasons why fish take much more freely in the spring and autumn than in the summer. At those times of the year water temperatures are appreciably lower with longer colder nights, the chance of frosts and maybe even snow melt from the hills. The air is therefore likely to be very much warmer than the water at that time of year except when a frosty wind is blowing or one with a touch of N or NE in it. Although it is quite possible to catch fish provided the air is only slightly warmer than the water and occasionally when both are the same temperature, it is very rare indeed to have success if the balance is tilted the slightest bit the other way. This condition applies particularly during the summer, and very often I think it is the sole factor why many anglers fishing in seemingly perfect conditions have blank days without moving or touching a fish. Very often I have heard anglers complaining that they could not understand why they were not catching anything, but if they had carried a thermometer and taken the temperature of the air and the water this would have been readily explained.

There are certain weather conditions which I regard as peculiarly favourable or unfavourable. The first of these is when snow is falling. This (usually) only occurs in the early months of the year and when snow starts to fall the air usually warms up significantly. Some of the best day's sport you could ever hope for have been in snowstorms. The only exception to this is when snow falls out of a freezing NE airstream and is that fine hard type the size of a pinhead, similar to very fine hail. Contrary to the success that so often attends a snowstorm, I have practically always found that thundery, heavy atmospheric conditions are usually hopeless. I think that you really have a very slim chance on heavy thundery days, but I have often seen fish come back on to the take as soon as the storm has broken and the atmosphere has cleared. The other time when fishing is invariably bad is when a sudden frost falls in the evening, particularly early in the year. This, when it happens, always ruins that magic period just before dusk sets in, and the same condition can also spoil evening and night fishing for sea trout. If you see a mist starting to rise from the water I would advise you to go home because in these conditions the air/water temperature gap is always wrong.

There are two other main factors of course which govern success on the river bank: wind and water. I will deal with wind first because it is not such a large object. We all know the old adage:

When the wind is in the North
The fisherman goes not forth
When the wind is in the East
Tis no good to man nor beast
When the wind is in the South
Blows the hook to the fishes mouth
When the wind is in the West
The fishing is at its best.

I am not a great supporter of this old angling adage and I prefer to think of wind as being either upstream or downstream. Many fishermen dislike an upstream wind, but unless this is a wind out of the N or NE, cold and harsh, which drops the air temperature radically, there is no valid reason why this should be adverse for angling. Indeed I would say that most upstream winds blowing up against the current will ruffle the surface of the stiller pools when the river is low. This allows these areas which otherwise would have been unfishable to be backed up and this can be a very successful way of fishing. Even on the Naver, which flows due north, a reasonable north wind can be an enormous benefit. I have known many experienced people who adjudge an upstream wind that puts a six inch wave on the still pools to be as beneficial as a six inch rise in water level and I fully agree with them. Gusty winds in any direction are a nuisance, particularly those which run across the surface of the water creating cat's paws and are generally unfavourable as regards fish taking. However, I think that this probably affects loch fishing much more than on a river.

Water conditions, and by that I mean the height of a river, is the other more important factor which can make or break a fishing holiday. Ideal conditions, of course, are a high to medium high river that is settled and dropping slowly. These are the conditions that every experienced fisherman hopes for. The entire length of his beat will be in good condition. And the angler can therefore pick up a fish anywhere on the beat with the best chances in the renowned taking lies in the main pools or resting places. These conditions also draw fish both from out of the sea and from downstream beats, and therefore the fisherman has an excellent chance of casting over fish that have not seen a lure before or that have changed pools. In both these cases the chances of success are greatly enhanced.

As the water level drops, fish are less inclined to ascend a river and the angler is then fishing over resident stock that has been left in the holding pools and as these fish become staler and staler the chances of success correspondingly decrease. These conditions can be particularly trying in the spring, especially if there is insufficient flow in the river to allow the angler to fish with a large enough fly. When this happens, the fisherman just has to pray for a strong upstream wind which will enable him to back up the still part of the holding pools and this method will also allow him to use much larger flies. In the summer, however, a fly fisher has more chance as he can then either use very small flies on a trout rod, fish with a floating line, or try dibbling or skating a dropper on the surface. Also because of the long hours of daylight he can then fish at differing times of the day. I personally would choose to fish before breakfast as then the air/water temperature gap is most likely to be favourable and also in the last hour and a half before the sun sets. In the summer, although the air/water temperature gap may not be favourable, fish seem to move out of the deeper waters of the pool into the fast flowing runs at the head or neck of a pool, where they are more catchable and more likely to take the fly.

There is another water condition when a lot of fisherman do not bother to fish – when the river is in torrential spate. I think that this can be a grave mistake, but it does depend on how dirty the river has become. If the river is too coloured then I would agree that there is little point in fishing but even in a bank high flood, if this has not occurred, there are chances and you have to go looking for the quiet corners into which the fish will have moved. Ironically enough these are usually very close and tucked into the bank. In a full spate the angler can catch fish casting the shortest of lines. An experienced ghillie who knows the river at all heights is a great help under these conditions.

When the river is rising then I would say it is unlikely that any fisherman will be very successful. There are, as in all salmon fishing, exceptions to this rule. The first is just at the beginning of a rise, particularly after a prolonged period of low water when, if the angler is fishing over fish at that precise moment, he is almost certain to move a fish to his fly. However, this magic moment usually lasts for less than half an hour and by the time you have landed your fish the optimum taking time will have passed. This rising river can apply particularly early in the year, when snow melting on the hills will cause the river to rise slowly in the late afternoon or evening. Very often in those early months anglers will suddenly be successful after a fruitless morning and early afternoon as soon as the river starts to rise and for an appreciable while after-wards. Certainly in my experience this taking period at that time of the year lasts much longer, and I have often been successful for two or three hours in the late afternoon, stopped only by the onset of darkness which has forced us to leave the river.

However, it is a fact that a long drawn out steady rise in the water level, or a fast rising river after a heavy spate offer poor angling conditions. Sometimes when this happens fish will not look at anything that is presented to them, while at other times the odd fish will either rise or pull the fly, but very few take properly. As a result of the fish that you do move under these conditions a good number are hooked and lost, or just pricked. I have heard many theories put forward as to why this should be. The main two are that fish are sickened by the increased turbidity of the water, or that they are impelled to move on upstream by the rise in the water level and therefore their thoughts are concentrated into the urge to reach their spawning grounds. No doubt both these arguments have some merit.

After all that I would say that there is only one absolutely certain rule in salmon fishing and that is that the only time you will not catch a salmon is when you are not fishing! At all other times, whatever the water or weather conditions, there is always some chance of catching a fish however remote this may be.

In the past, people who owned and lived beside their own water and knew their fishing intimately could pick and choose the time at which they wanted to fish. They knew the weather and water conditions when they were most likely to succeed and therefore they tended to fish at those times, or if they could not fish them-selves asked friends to fish for them instead. This very often meant that the river was fished sparingly but effectively and fish were seldom hammered in adverse or low water conditions. Obviously the catch to effort ratio was good, and the better the potential of the actual beat the better this ratio showed. In modern times, however, with the escalation in demand for fishing coupled with the exhorbitant cost of running the fishing, few are in the position to run their fishing rights in this way.

Generally most fishery owners keep certain weeks of the year for their own use and let the remaining fishing to tenants on either a fortnightly or weekly basis. In this way everyone is really in the hands of the weather, and if you happen to be lucky and fish at a time when the river is in good order then you will generally be successful. At other times the river may be out of ply and you may have a totally blank week or fortnight. As a general rule, it is best to try to stick to the same time over a period of years, as then your mean catch will average out, whereas if you chop and change you may miss out on the one year when your beat has a bonanza.

I would say that if, on average, an angler catches two fish in a six day week with a number of lost fish and pulls, then he is doing well and can be thankful. But this does depend on the skill and perseverance of the individual angler, and everyone should remember that salmon fishing is an unpredictable challenge, sometimes frustrating, sometimes unexpectedly rewarding but success rarely comes easily. Patience and perseverance have a lot to do with it.

Beginner's Luck

Beginner's Luck! What a splendid idea. The tyro walks in with the only fish of the day and we can put it all down to the smile of Dame Fortune. I am sure that anyone who has fished for any length of time can quote instances where that has happened.

But is it always just luck? Possibly. Personally I am unconvinced for I have seen too many instances of 'beginner's luck' to feel inclined to give Dame Fortune credit on every occasion. I think that it would serve all salmon fishermen better if they looked at some of the instances they know and see whether they could draw some lessons from them. Let me tell a story or two from my own experience to show what I mean.

Some years ago I was studying agriculture at Llysfasi Farm Institute in North Wales, which was not far from our home in the Llangollen valley. Often I used to go home for the weekend and one weekend I invited a girl who was taking the same course to come home with me. It was in April; she was very keen to catch a salmon and asked if I could show her how to fish.

Generally the chances would have been good, for Argoed, our beat, was a good one in the spring provided the weather had been mild enough for the fish to ascend the weir at Erbistock, some miles downstream. That spring had certainly been mild but the week before had been wet, and after heavy rainfall the Welsh Dee is often very coloured as it flows through agricultural land. That Friday night when we reached home the river was still flowing high and dirty, and on Saturday morning it was still too high and coloured for there to be any hope of catching a fish on the fly.

Spinning it would have to be, so after breakfast we went to the old stables where the rods were kept and I found a spinning rod with one of the old Silex Easy-Cast reels which, in those days, were the easiest for beginners to use. Our house on the Dee stood on the top of a high wooded bank which sometime in the last century had started to be undermined by a series of high floods. To avert this danger my grandfather had been forced to build a stone break-water along the bottom of the bank. The breakwater was nearly half a mile long and had a flat top four feet wide down its entire length. He also had to build a small gauge railway to carry the material to the site, and after the work was finished he had the railway line replaced by a long flight of stone steps, interspersed with terraced paths. At the foot of the steps he built a summer house, beside what then became known as the 'Summer- house Pool'.

As we walked down the 233 steps to the river's edge that Saturday I cannot say that I felt very optimistic about our chances. The river was too high and coloured, the day itself was cold, grey and damp. I thought that after an hour or two my companion's enthusiasm for fishing would be finished almost as soon as it had begun. But I am an optimist by nature and I did my best to belittle the conditions of the day.

The Summer-house pool is about two hundred yards long. For the first one hundred and thirty yards or so the stream bears in against the home bank, and is kept away from the main break-water by rock revetment works placed there when the breakwater was being built. After this the stream swings out towards the centre of the pool and at this point a lone tree stands on the landward side of the breakwater. From there to the tail of the pool there is a lovely smooth glide – an ideal taking place in high water as fish ascending the pool below, the Run, rest in the glide after coming through the fast water below. At this point the breakwater stands about six feet above the level of the river and there are only a few places along its entire length which provides a good enough foothold for a ghillie to get down to the water's edge to land a fish. This was an added complication in playing a fish.

As the river was so high I chose a large black and orange minnow from my box and I also attached a spiral lead to the trace some way above the minnow. I knew that if there were any fish they would be lying deep and there was little danger of my companion's catching the bottom, as there were no bad snags in that part of the pool. I wanted to leave the most likely part of the pool until she had mastered the art of casting so we started at the top of the pool and, after a time, she began to get the minnow a reasonable distance across the river. She persisted with great determination and it did not seem to matter to me that a number of her casts were rather upstream of square, for the current was

11

running so fast that the stream straightened out the minnow very quickly.

After an hour we moved down to the tail of the pool and just as her minnow swung round above the rapids I saw the line tighten and the battle was on. Looking back over the years I can say that if ever a salmon behaved impeccably this one did. It was so well hooked that it survived my pupil's clamped hand on the reel, and if you are fishing with a novice, this is one of the things to watch out for if, and when, they hook their first fish. It allowed itself to be walked up for seventy yards and then be led quietly into the only backwater the whole length of the breakwater, where after a quarter of an hour I gaffed out a bright cock fish weighing just over eighteen pounds.

As there were still forty-five minutes before lunch we returned immediately to the tail of the pool. After another dozen casts again the line tightened and my pupil struck perfectly. This fish lay still for a minute and then took off in an unstoppable rush downstream into the rapids below. It was imperative to stop the fish in the one piece of quiet water at the tail of the Run, for if it ran through that pool there were trees at the head of the Major pool, the next pool downstream, and if the fish went as far as there we would lose it.

With these thoughts running through my mind I seized the rod from my pupil's hands and told her to follow me. As I ran downstream I moved the catch on the reel to the free position to give the fish as much slack line as possible. This worked as it so often does. (May I recommend this trick to all salmon fishermen who do not know it. If you want to stop a fish leaving a pool, drop your rod and give the fish as much slack as possible. Very often the fish will turn and can then be controlled. The only time not to do this is when you have a beaten fish rolling on the top of the water in a heavy stream.)

In this case the fish settled down in the right place so I passed the rod back with the instruction to be as hard on it as she could. I knew that the tackle was strong enough to stand the strain and I had to trust that the fish was really well hooked. Again all went well and a few minutes later I gaffed out a beautiful twenty-one pounds fresh run salmon, covered with sea lice.

Lunch was a hurried meal for my pupil could hardly wait to return to the taking spot. However the afternoon proved less productive. Despite several changes of minnow nearly two hours passed without a sign of a fish and, as a last resort, I decided to try the tail of another pool, the Pentre, which lay about a quarter of a mile upstream. As we walked up there I warned her that if she did hook a fish she would have to drop the point of her rod straight away and give the fish line, as there were trees lining the bank at the tail of the pool which meant that you couldn't follow any fish downstream. There is a ledge which runs along the side of the Pentre pool and we waded out on to it and started to fish the tail. Almost immediately she pulled a fish. After twenty minutes another took and rushed off down to the tail. My pupil slackened off line straight away and the fish turned upstream, but as it did so it snagged the line round a rock in the river some twenty yards below us. The fish then jumped and wrenched the hook from its mouth, a sad loss as the fish was around twenty pounds.

After I had replaced the spinning mount as the hooks had been straightened out, she cast again and first cast hooked yet another fish. This one behaved very placidly and was soon landed, a rather stale hen fish which weighed fourteen and a half pounds.

By now darkness had fallen and we returned home in triumph. My guest had had a day to remember, not merely three spring salmon on the first day she had ever had a salmon rod in her hands but all heavy fish, hooked in heavy water and landed under extremely difficult conditions. I thought at the time she had deserved her luck for she had shown determination, stamina, patience and willingness to listen to advice and obey instructions.

Shortly after that day I left agricultural college and went to live at Rosehall in Sutherland and I did not meet my guest for another eighteen years. Then, in 1966, Jennifer came to stay with my sister at Invercassley House, just across the river from where I lived. Again she showed an interest in fishing but she warned me that she had not touched a fishing rod since that day on the Welsh Dee some eighteen years ago. The Cassley is a fly-only river so after a short casting lesson on the lawn in front of the house we went to the river.

It was a nice mild day in the middle of March and the river, swollen with melting snow from the hills, had been running at a good height for several days, and during this time we had caught a number of fish. I decided I would take her up the right-hand bank to the Round pool, for at that height of water the fish would be lying close in under the bank and she would not have to cast any great length of line. As we walked up the river, Hamish, one of the ghillies, called across that he had seen a running fish show at the tail of the Round pool but that he had not moved anything to his flies.

I started Jennifer off at the 'cup-stone' at the head of the pool to try a few casts from there, but this part of the pool was a bit high so we moved down about twenty yards to the next rock to fish the tail of the pool. I thought that this would be the best chance we had for a fish but Jennifer made several good casts from the rock, all nicely laid on the water with no result, and I was just thinking that we were going to be unlucky when she made a really bad cast, everything landing in a heap just seven yards from the bank. As there was plenty of current to straighten the line I did not tell her to cast again and to my astonishment, as the fly swung into the bank a fish took solidly.

It would be nice to relate that my pupil's expertise in playing a salmon had survived the passing years. It had not; but it did not matter as this fish, like the ones on the Dee, was really well hooked and in a few minutes a lovely ten pound salmon was lying on the bank.

Shortly after this day Jennifer and I got married so for me those days form a unique double of good fortune, but for the purposes of this book I think they teach an important lesson.

On the Dee I must make it clear that for a good part of the day Jennifer and I were sharing the spinning rod. I had every bit as good a chance of catching a fish as she did and in fact I never had an offer. I was an experienced fisher and I was casting square across the stream (as would be recommended practice at that height of water) and releasing some line as the minnow hit the surface to help it to sink. The river was very high. When Jennifer was fishing her casting was not nearly so regular as mine. On some occasions she strayed a good long way upstream and she always continued to release line as I had instructed her whether she cast square across the river or not. Sometimes when she cast a long way upstream her minnow would have been very deep indeed by the time it started to fish and I realise now that every time she hooked a fish it was from one of her upstream casts.

On the second day the Round pool had already been fished by one of the ghillies who is a masterly fisherman, even if from the other bank. Jennifer had already covered the fish she hooked quite nicely on two or three occasions. You can say, if you want to, that the fish had only just entered the pool and the cast that caught it was the first one that covered it. Maybe, but I don't think so. The cast that caught the fish was a real dog's breakfast, all of a heap and barely more than a rod's length from the bank. By the time the current had straightened the line the fly would have been well down, far deeper than any of her previous casts and far deeper than Hamish's fly from the opposite bank. It is my opinion that the depth at which the fly and the minnow were fished on both those two days was the main factor in Jennifer's 'beginner's luck'.

Let me tell two more stories which, even if not of beginner's luck, show how the most unorthodox presentation can catch fish. The first one happened on the Crow's Nest pool on the Cassley where, when the light is right, you can look far down into the water and clearly see not only the fish you are fishing over, but also the movement of your fly. This can be very exciting. However to fish this pool properly, standing high above the water, you have to move your rod square to the river after you have cast, and handline the fly to make it swim sedately across the pool away from the fish. On the day in question I took an old friend from Wales to fish the pool and I warned him about this before he started. You fish the pool from a rock ledge high above the water and when we got there we could see several fish lying on the far side of the stream right in the best taking place. To my horror the first cast he made landed in a great heap right on top of the fish. My friend then made no attempt at all to get in contact with his fly which sank deeper and deeper into the pool, so by the time the current caught the fly it was about four feet down in the water and literally inches away from the noses of the fish. Then, just as the current caught the bag in the line and started to whip the fly away from the fish, one of them shot forward and grabbed it. The fish was landed and my friend turned to me in all innocence and asked whether he had fished the pool correctly. I had not the heart to say that he had made a complete mess of it so I just nodded my head. Besides, who was I to criticise someone who had just caught a fish – even if in such an unorthodox fashion?

I would like to remind all experienced salmon fishermen and women that the salmon is the most unpredictable fish, and 'you can never tell what he will do or when he will do it'. Of course, nine times out of ten, if you can cast a good line and cover your water regularly you will catch more fish than the person who cannot achieve this. But there are times when salmon will not respond to what one would call the orthodox method and then it can pay to try a variety of different presentations. For this reason if I make a really bad cast I always fish it out. I always back up a pool because I believe that salmon can be stirred into action by the fly presented in this manner; in the summer I always try dibbling or fishing with a riffling hitch and if conditions are right in high water I will cast square across the river and try to fish my fly or minnow really deep in the water. And, just occasionally I will try 'bombing' the fish.

I came across this last tactic almost by accident fishing on the Shin early one May. I was fishing with Bill MacDonald, the ghillie, from the Falls pool down to the tail of the Rocky Cast. We saw no sign of any fish moving all day but we could see three fish lying in the taking place in a pool called the Shoulder of Cromarty. We spent some time fishing for them but three changes of fly brought no response.

On our way back upstream at the end of the morning we decided to try these fish again with a larger fly, in this case a 2/0 Hairy Mary. The Shoulder of Cromarty is fished from a rocky ledge which starts about five feet above the water and then ascends diagonally so that by the time you reach the end of the fishable water you are standing about twenty feet above the river. In the spring when the water is clear you can see right down into the pool and every fish and stone shows clearly. These three fish were lying far back in the pool. I covered them several times but they took no interest in my fly whatsoever. Billy MacDonald then suggested that I try a squarer cast to try and get the fly to them at a different angle. Still no effect; but when I tried to repeat the cast my fly caught momentarily on a birch twig behind me and then landed with a great splash right on top of the fish. As I tried to regain contact with my fly the smallest of the fish swam downstream after it and then took it with a great wallop on the way back.

Since then I have used this tactic with success on several occasions, and I think that it does sometimes wake up fish who would otherwise have stayed at the bottom of the river taking no notice of any lure whatsoever.

There is another occasion when you can use this tactic. Sometimes you can move a fish which either misses or fails to take it properly. If this fish does not come to a smaller fly or any other change that you care to try, as a last resort you can put on a much larger fly and casting square to the fish bang the fly down on its nose. Strip the fly back quickly and sometimes you will provoke the salmon into renewed and, one hopes, more accurate action.

So let us think then about the beginner whether he or she be fishing with fly or minnow. Sometimes they will make a good cast, sometimes their direction will be awry and blown by the wind, or misdirected and will be upstream rather than down and across: some casts will land in a heap only a few yards across the river. And I would suggest that those true examples of 'beginner's luck', and by that I mean the occasions when the beginner walks in with the only fish of the day, are the days when the beginner has inadvertently perhaps presented his fly or minnow to the fish in the way that the fish happen to want it on that particular day. I do not decry Dame Fortune, I look to her for many future favours, but I think she would be kinder to all fishermen if they were more adventurous and less conservative.

The Birth of a Fly

I have never been a fly tier, mainly I think because my hands are rather like a bunch of bananas, but I have always been interested in the various patterns of salmon flies and I have admired those who can produce such beautiful things as salmon flies with apparently so little effort.

One of the things that interested me was the effectiveness or otherwise of the Collie Dog pattern soon after it was invented. As most people know the prototype was merely a snip of hair from the tail of a black collie whipped on to the plain shank of a No. 1 hook. The prototype was developed either on single shank hooks or tubes, and tied with bodies of silver, red, or red and gold. All these dressings were successful. I found them more successful than the traditional flies and I used them constantly but I noticed, particularly early in the season, that the Collie dressings were not as successful except when the water temperature rose above 42°F. I did not really know why this should be but it was a factor that stuck in my mind.

One day early in March I was fishing the Oykel with Peter Campbell, a great friend of mine, as my ghillie. The river had been high with melting snow for several days and early that morning heavy rain had started to fall. I knew that the river was bound to rise soon after we started fishing. Our beat was from the Rock pool down to the tail of Langwell, and we started at the head of Langwell as it seemed that we might only have one opportunity to fish that bit of water that day before the river rose too much. Straight away I hooked and landed a small spring fish, but by the time the fish was on the bank the river was obviously rising fast and we had no other offers, although we tried all the flies we could think of. It was obviously the one fish caught just on the first rise of the river. By lunchtime our beat was virtually unfishable and the only places were on either side of the boat in the Rock pool, the lower half of

18

the Stone pool, and below the bridge at Langwell right at the tail of the pool. As we lunched at the hut on the Stone pool we discussed our chances and decided that the only hope would be if the river stopped rising and started to settle. The constant downpour of the morning had now ceased, and looking up the Rappach valley we could see blue sky and occasional bright intervals in the midst of the grey and overcast sky. We put sticks in the river at the water's edge to see whether the river was beginning to hold or even drop a little.

Peter went to his fishing bag and took out several bulky tins for, he said, we would be better employed in tying some flies than casting when there was no chance of success. He asked me for some suggestions. I said that I had wanted for a long time to produce a version of the Collie Dog which was more colourful and why should we not try and incorporate the two colours that I had always found to be the most effective in spring fishing, yellow and crimson. We therefore decided to have a fly the top half of which would have a red or crimson body, and the bottom half a yellow body. The fly would have the traditional collie wing, and there should be some yellow hair at the tail of the fly protruding from the yellow silk binding.

Leaving Peter to work on this suggestion I went out to look at the river and I was pleased to see that it had not risen since my last inspection half an hour before. I then had a cast or two at the tail of the Stone pool and saw a running fish move right in the tail of the pool which was good news. On my return to the hut I found the fly tied exactly to my specifications and I then suggested that Peter should give it a red head just like old Doctor flies to finish it off. When this was done Peter left the fly in his vice to dry and we set off to the tail of Langwell pool to try our luck.

When we got there I switched out a short length of line just below the guy wires supporting the bridge and to my amazement I saw a fish come up at the fly, a big black and yellow tube, and move to it without touching it. Next cast nothing happened, so I changed my fly to a big four inch Collie and next cast the fish grabbed it. The following two hours were extremely hectic. Peter and I had another fish each in Langwell and we also landed six kelts between us. Then on our return to the Stone pool, I got two more fresh fish and Peter caught one and lost two.

As darkness fell two tired and happy people returned to the car carrying the seven fish that we had caught between us, the new fly almost fogotten in our excitement. However as we parted Peter handed me our new pattern of fly and suggested that we should call it the Tadpole as it had a short stubby body and a long tail.

Next day I was fishing on the Rosehall beat of the Cassley, and I showed the new fly to Willie Mackay, my keeper. The Cassley was running at three foot six inches, an ideal height for March and I could tell by the look on Willie's face that he did not think much of my new invention. I still had the Collie Dog on my rod which had been so successful the day before so I decided not to change it. We started fishing at the Round pool from the field, although that pool was really too high to fish from the bank apart from a few casts from the rocks right at the tail. I moved nothing there and nothing in the Run below, but Willie took a fish at the tail of the Round pool on a big black and yellow tube.

After that we moved down to the Upper Platform pool which I thought would be an absolute certainty that day at that height of water. But I had no move at all when I fished it down first with the Collie, and Willie had nothing when he followed me down with his tube fly. While he was fishing I tied on the Tadpole for its first outing and I dangled the fly in the water below the wooden platform to see how it looked in the water. I was pleasantly surprised by its appearance and when Willie had finished I started fishing, lengthening my cast yard by yard to the 'black boil' lie in the centre of the pool. As I covered the lie a fish took and soon the first fish caught on a Tadpole was on the bank.

Willie then went down to the Lower Platform pool while I fished the Upper Platform again and I caught a second fish at the tail of the pool. Willie was so absorbed with his fishing that he never noticed I was playing a fish, so I took my time and soon beached a nice twelve pound fish on the rock just below the Platform. I then tried the pool a third time and even backed it up but I had no further joy.

When I went down to the Lower Platform pool I found that Willie had had no success, but when I fished it I caught a third fish right at the tail of the pool. As I landed this fish I noticed that the binding had become frayed so I took the fly off to save it further damage. We ended the day with nine fish but I often wonder what our bag might have been had I had a good supply of the Tadpole that day. That night I went up the glen to tell Peter of the success of the new fly and he promised that he would tie me up a supply of that pattern in various sizes. The Tadpole has since become our most successful fly on the Cassley, throughout the year, but

20

The Run – River Cassley
A most productive fly pool.

particularly in the spring before the water temperatures rise above 42°F and I know that it is used by many fishermen with great effect throughout Scotland.

At the time I don't suppose that either Peter or I thought that we had produced anything other than an attractive looking fly. In fact with what are really only minor alterations to an established killing pattern, we achieved a transformation in its effectiveness in early spring when water temperatures are below 42°F. And I have found that the Tadpole will kill well fished in all sizes throughout the year.

Another spectacular change in the fortunes of a fly came with the changes made by Willie Gunn to the established black and orange, or black and yellow tubes which have been used with great effect for a number of years by many fishermen. Willie just mixed black, yellow and orange hair together when tying his tube and more or less copied the old body of a Thunder and Lightning. The general effect is of a sombre fly which reminds me of the old Thunder and Lightning dressing but it has made a spectacular change to the effectiveness of the fly which now bears his name. The Willie Gunn fished in all sizes in the modern Waddington range is one of the most successful flies there is and I know that a number of fishermen, fishing especially in the large rivers of the south of Scotland in the spring, have found that the Willie Gunn is more effective than the devon minnows and other spinning baits which they normally use. Many anglers have found that this fly fished on a fly rod is far more effective than any bait and have abandoned their spinning rods so that they can use it. Certainly if I was thinking of new flies I would be looking to copy the bodies and capture the essence of some of the old favourites such as the Jock Scott, Mar Lodge and Black Doctor dressed with hair wings, and I am sure that they would catch many fish.

Fly Patterns – Do they matter?

A number of years ago I was asked to go and fish on the Laxford. My father and the late Bendore, Duke of Westminster were friends as we lived close to Eaton Hall and I used to ghillie for the Duke when he came over to fish our beat on the Welsh Dee. As things turned out the Duke died suddenly just before I was due to go over to the West coast and all fishing on the estate was postponed until after his funeral. However, shortly afterwards the factor, Colonel Neilson, rang me at Rosehall and arranged for me to go and fish for a day.

On the morning of the date we drove over from Rosehall and I picked up Billy Scobie, the ghillie, who was to accompany me that day. We started at the top of the beat just below the Lodge and when I had put up my rod Billy looked at my fly boxes to select a fly. He wanted to put on a shrimp fly, a favourite fly on the Laxford, but we were never very successful with these on the Cassley and I did not have one. However I did have two rather maroon-coloured Usk Grubs which I had been given, and as they were deemed to be the right size I put on one of these instead. When we started fishing it was obvious that the river was in excellent order and as it had not been fished for several days everything should have been in our favour. I started at the Top Pool. This has a narrow run at the head of the pool which then turns left-handed into the main pool. Just above the bend I hooked a good fish which weighed seventeen pounds when Scobie netted it out. A nice start to the day.

I fished the pool down again and shortly landed another fish of twelve pounds which had just come into the river as it was covered with sea lice. The rest of the pool and the Lower Top pool yielded nothing save two small sea trout and we then went down to a pool called Mrs Cook. There the fish lay on the far side of the river where the current flowed, and as I fished it down carefully I got a fierce underwater pull from a fish, but on tightening I was surprised to get only a momentary contact with the fish as I was certain it had taken firmly. No matter, I fished on down and moments later I had another pull. At this point I decided to examine my fly and I was annoyed when I reeled in to find that the shank of the hook had sheered just at the bottom of the dressing, a clean break which obviously had happened when the fish had taken so fiercely at the top of the pool. This was the first time this had ever happened to me although I could remember losing a very heavy fish on the Oykel in Upper Scolgeach on a No. 4 Garry Dog when the hook straightened out almost completely.

However at the time I though little of it and I tried several other patterns of fly in which Scobie had great faith, but we did not move a fish in any of the three pools we had already fished or in the Island or Corner pool, although the latter was a great favourite of Scobie's. We then went down to the Duke's pool where I was assured I was bound to catch or move something, but again, in spite of trying two or three flies including the favoured shrimp fly, the fish remained completely uninterested although a number could be seen moving in the pools.

After lunch we moved down to the Duchess pool, an attractive rocky pool which was fished from a concrete walkway which projected out into the river and ran down the stream parallel to the left bank, but apart from seeing an adder on the path, we had no excitements. By now we were pretty puzzled. At first that morning the fish had seemed really keen and we had moved several almost straight away. Now it was as if nothing we could do would interest them in any way.

As we discussed this we retraced our steps to the Duke's pool and when we got there I made Scobie fish it down again with his shrimp fly while I tied on my last Usk Grub, although apart from its rather claret body it was identical to the shrimp fly that Scobie had on. As I started fishing behind him I really thought that it was a forlorn hope but to my surprise a fish took me at the tail of the neck of the pool and after a brief fight we netted out a small grilse covered with sea lice.

We then caught two more fish in that pool, both on the Usk Grub, and it seemed to us that for some strange reason the Usk Grub was the only fly the fish would take that day. This was confirmed when we reached the Corner pool which Scobie fished down first with a favourite pattern of his which produced no result, and fishing after him I caught another small fish of eight pounds. There was no doubt in our minds that this was one of those rare days when the pattern of fly makes all the difference and as we made our way back to the Top pool we decided that we would really put the matter to the test beyond any probable or possible shadow of doubt.

When we reached the pool we each fished with three different flies, making six fishings of the pool in all. We tried the shrimp fly which was usually so successful and two other flies which had claret-coloured bodies, the Gordon and the Poynder, and all the flies were the same size as the killer Usk Grub. Then, seventh time down the pool, I tied on the Usk Grub, and just where I had killed my first fish of the morning there was a big swirl and I was into a good heavy fish. As this fish raced round the pool it jumped twice and the second time my fly came back to me, broken in the same place as the first Usk Grub that morning. Well, we fished on until our allotted time, but never another offer did we get and I suppose that had we had a number of Usk Grubs on that day dressed on reliable irons we would have had a record day. Now thirty years later I am glad we didn't, for if we had, we would never have experimented with so many different flies and would never have been in the position to prove that on that day the fish would only take one pattern of fly, which I submit we did.

What are the lessons that can be drawn from this and how important is the pattern of the fly as opposed to the size. I know that there are a number of anglers, including some of the most famous names in salmon fishing, who believe that pattern is of relatively little importance but I think that there are times when it is a good deal more important than we like to think. Of course it matters far more when the fish are a bit sticky for some reason or other, for when they are taking freely they will take almost anything that is thrown at them.

There are several aspects of fly patterns. In the olden days when flies were flies we would fish with the Green Highlander, Yellow Torrish, Durham Ranger or Childers when we used bright flies; Thunder and Lightning, Black Doctor, Jock Scott and Black Dog for the duller colours; and Mar Lodge, Dusty Miller and Silver Grey for the silver-bodied flies. My favourite fly at that time was a Mar Lodge and one year I fished exclusively with this pattern and the number of fish that I caught was almost exactly the same as usual. When I fished on our beat of the Welsh Dee I generally used a Silver Wilkinson, Yellow Peril or Poynder, but these flies were practically useless on the Cassley. Needless to say, in my youth I would not really believe this and spent many hours on the Cassley fishing with these flies, but I doubt if I caught more than six fish with them on that river while I suppose that over 50% of my fish on the Welsh Dee would have been taken with these patterns.

When I started fishing on the other rivers in the north of Scotland I was asked often by the ghillies with whom I fished to put on a Garry Dog. This proved to be a successful fly but when I tried it on the Cassley it was no use at all and I never caught a fish on it. Then one day I was in Inverness talking to Donnie Macdougall, the fly tier at MacLeay and Sons, and he showed me a variation of the traditional Garry Dog tied with a slightly orange hair wing instead of the traditional yellow, and gold tinsel instead of silver on the body. This version of the fly proved very successful on the Cassley and until we abandoned the old single hooked flies in favour of tubes, I would say that it was our most successful fly in all sizes throughout the year. Time and again I would re-test it against the traditional tying of the Garry Dog but always the same result. And it just shows how sometimes a marginal alteration in the pattern of fly can make all the difference.

The other thing to bear in mind is that some patterns of fly are definitely more effective at different times of the year. To my mind this applies particularly to the Mar Lodge, a good enough fly at any time but at its best in May during the annual smolt migration. I remember one spring when the Cassley was at a perfect height for our beat. I had a meeting that day and had asked four friends to fish and so I told MacKay to leave me a place below the bridge which I would fish at tea time when I returned. I started fishing at the Crag pool at four p.m. and had a big 9/0 Mar Lodge on my rod which I did not bother to change as the river was running very high. Almost immediately I caught a fish and then I moved down to the Dyke pool below where I caught another. Willie arrived as I was playing this fish and when he had netted it I asked how the others had fared. To my surprise he said that they were blank and had not moved a fish all day. Asked whether they had tried the Mar Lodge he admitted that they hadn't, and I suggested that he should return to them and that they should try this fly as they were fishing the best of the water.

When we met up at the end of the day they had caught five fish between them, all on the Mar Lodge and all after four p.m. I think that this is another day when they might well have had a blank day had I not returned, simply because they had not changed their flies enough and failed to try all the old favourites.

Other flies as well as the Mar Lodge had particular times of the year when they were successful. The Green Highlander, although a good fly at any time, seemed to me to be most successful when the trees were just coming into leaf in the spring. Another seasonal fly was the Frau Diavolo, a fly which saved many a blank on the Carron in Easter Ross. This fly worked best in the gin-clear, cold waters of early spring and I never had much success with it after the water temperture rose above 42°F.

Nowadays I nearly always fish with one of the long-tailed varieties of fly and generally use the Collie Dog, Tadpole or Willie Gunn in a variety of sizes. The one thing I have found is that the Collie is only really effective when the water temperature rises above 42°F. It will kill fish in very cold water temperatures but I have found that the Tadpole is much more effective early in the season. When I fish the Cassley I very often make my ghillie carry a rod and fish alternate pools with me, as early in the season I believe in fishing each pool quickly and then returning to it again, sometimes as many as two or three times in the day. When we fish as a pair one of us will fish with a Tadpole and one a big Collie Dog, and it is remarkable how often one of us will kill the whole bag on one day and on another day the other. When the fish are being single-minded about the fly they will take it is very rare for the unlucky rod to get even a single offer, and there is absolutely no apparent reason why this should be so.

In the autumn I think that reddish or orange flies are best, and if the river is very peat-stained, I think that a fly with a gold body is best. Somehow the gold-bodied flies seem to show up best in peaty water. At that time of year I would choose from the following: General Practitioner, Member, President, Dunkeld or Cinnamon and Gold. I do believe that the body of the fly is as important as the wing, and as a fly twists and turns in the current of the river the body glints and this draws the attention of the fish to it. This I am sure is particularly so on a dull day or in coloured water. For this reason I think that it is a mistake to fish with tube flies that are too heavily dressed, as many of them seem to be. I always try and get my tube flies dressed just with the hair on the top of the body as a top wing leaving the underside exposed. Alternatively use only tubes that are very lightly dressed like some of the modern

Waddington flies as this allows ample light to penetrate through to the body. This small detail can make a substantial difference to the effectiveness of the fly, and at times even to use a gold or silver treble in preference to a bronze or black one can make the difference between success and failure.

Of course there is a complete divergence here between assumed or general practice and theory. General practice says, and quite rightly, that on many occasions it doesn't really matter what you fish with, that size is more important than pattern, and the most important thing for the angler is to fish with a fly in which he or she has confidence. I agree with all this, I agree with it totally, but at the same time I would like to propose an unprovable theory which a lifetime's experience fishing for salmon convinces me is more often true than most anglers would admit. I think that an analogy with the brown trout fishing is appropriate. If you fish for trout on an river very often you will only be successful with an exact pattern of the insect on which the trout is feeding. We have all seen it and experienced it. Salmon are different, of course they are. They have changed their habitat many times in the course of their life before returning to the river to spawn. They have journeyed many hundreds of mile through different seas and they will have fed on a large variety of food sources.

When they return to the river of their birth they cease to feed, and the angler is faced with the problem of trying to stimulate the memory of former feeding patterns. Well, memory is a funny thing, and sometimes it works imperfectly and at other times it works very well indeed, and it is when the memory of the salmon is working at its best that some detail of the fly, or one type of pattern is taken to the exclusion of all others. On these occasions I would submit that detail can make just as much difference in salmon fishing as it can on the trout stream, but I accept that I can't prove this.

It has always seemed to me that the old-fashioned flies such as the Jock Scott, which were dressed with such extravagant and loving care, were devised with far more thought than is at first apparent. If you swim any of these patterns in the water it is remarkable how lifelike they appear, just like the small fish that I am sure they were originally intended to be. It is noticeable that the gaudy patterns used mostly in the spring all had jungle cock feathers inserted on either side at the head of the fly to represent the eyes of the fish. The duller-hued patterns which were used in

Resting between casts – River Glass.

the height of summer did not have this embellishment as they were intended to represent the duller-hued plankton. This is an important point for when you fish with these flies you are fishing with something which hangs inert in the current, and does not, like a small fish, attempt to swim across it. This was the real point made by Arthur Wood when he 'invented' greased line fishing for salmon as the angler must mend his line and bring his fly across the current as slowly as possible.

Well all this is, in a way, rather academic. We all, or nearly all, fish with certain well tried patterns of hair-winged tube flies and the old fashioned salmon fly is a thing of the past. And I would say that the modern fly is more effective than the old-fashioned one, although I must admit that I have not ever made a contrived experiment of this over a sufficient time to prove it to myself one way or the other. However I do think that the comparatively few patterns found in the modern angler's fly box does mean that sometimes we will miss out on a day when the salmon want something special. I think that the day on the Laxford was a supreme example of this and I will end this discourse with another example.

One season on the Welsh Dee, in early May, the river was full of fish. The water level was dropping after a good spate and while the river was still at a good fishable height it was getting too low for fresh fish to run. The fish therefore had become stale in their lies and we had not killed a single fish for two days.

A friend of my father's was staying near Llangollen and he was going to fish for three days on the Welsh Dee: the first day on our beat at Argoed, and the next two days at Sun Bank and Feachan, two beats upstream of our water. When he arrived my father told him that prospects were not good and that the fish were very stiff. I was to accompany him as ghillie and guide and we set off. In the morning we fished from the Summer-house pool to the bottom of the beat, and although we tried all the favourite flies and all the best pools we caught nothing, although quite a number of good fish could be seen moving.

At lunchtime, as we sat and ate our lunch in front of the summerhouse, we discussed various aspects of fishing and what flies we should try. He told me that he had been fishing on the Wye and had been given a fly called a Haslam while he was there and had had great success with it. I suggested that he should try it now as we certainly weren't doing any good with anything else. When he produced it from his box I certainly wasn't impressed with it as it was rather like a Silver March Brown except for the hackle and yellow flash. We had already tried a Silver Grey, Mar Lodge and Silver Wilkinson without success and I couldn't see why the Haslam should succeed. Nevertheless he tied it on.

After lunch we fished the Summer-house pool again. He insisted I fish it down first which I did with a Mar Lodge and he came down after me. When I was about half way down the pool I heard a cry behind me and there was my father's friend into a fish. In due course I gaffed out a nice fish for him weighing seventeen and a half pounds. I then changed my fly to a Silver Grey of the same size as the Haslam he had on, and we went down to the Major pool. Again I fished the pool first and again when he came in after me he hooked and landed a fish, this time a salmon of twenty-one pounds.

That was the extent of our success that day but in the next two days he caught two fish at Sun Bank and three at Feachan, all on the Haslam, when neither of these two beats had had a fish for several days previously. Was it just luck? I doubt it and I subsequently found the Haslam to be a great standby when fish were dour.

I think that the moral of all this for the fisherman is to change your fly frequently. Always try something new particularly when conditions look right but for some reason the fish are being stiff. Maybe it is one of those days when they will only take one pattern of fly, and that a pattern not normally considered. If this is the case only constant changes will give you any chance of finding the right fly and saving the blank.

A Question of Confidence

One summer Jennifer and I were asked to fish on the Castle Grant beat of the Spey for two days. I knew the beat well as I had acted as a consultant for the fishery there for a number of years but I had never fished it at that time of year. We drove over the night before and prior to starting for the river I put up our rods and tied on a No. 7 Hairy Mary on Jennifer's. On my own rod I tied my customary No. 9 Hairy Mary on the dropper with a one inch long-haired Tadpole in the tail position.

Now this was, I admit, rather a large fly for the prevailing conditions. The river was fairly low. It was in the height of summer and a much smaller fly would be normal. At that time the long-haired flies, such as the Tadpole and Collie Dog were relatively unknown and untried but I had found them to be most effective at all heights of water and that when you used them it was best to fish with much larger sizes than would be normal in summer conditions.

When we met at the fishing hut that morning my host introduced me to the ghillie as 'the renowned striker from the north'. This was, I think, a bit tactless of him but the ghillie responded by saying, 'if he strikes here he is going to have a disappointing time' and he compounded his displeasure by marching over to our rods and when he came to mine he said, 'we don't fish droppers here and what is more your tail fly is far too large.'

In a long career on the banks of many rivers I have only on the oddest of occasions met with anything except politeness and courtesy from a ghillie, and this particular ghillie, I can only assume, wanted to impress me with his knowledge of his beat.

However these remarks merely made me more determined to succeed and prove to him how wrong he was. I therefore made no comment and Jennifer and I went up to fish Polwick and Greenbank. Polwick is probably the most famous holding pool on this beat of the Spey. It is a wide pool on a left-hand bend with a wide, fast stream flowing in to the head and deep water on the right bank as the river sweeps down and round on a left-hand bend under the main road and down Speyside. In the summer it fishes best from the left bank but at certain heights of water it can also fish well from the right-hand bank. Greenbank is a long smooth glide, almost a continuation of Polwick, with the main stream under the right bank. It is best fished from the left bank with the angler throwing a long line across to the far side of the river, letting his fly swing across the smooth glide.

Jennifer started fishing Polwick while I went upstream to fish the Sluggan of Polwick, a fast stream which at that height of water was rather on the high side. There was nothing doing there so I came down to join Jennifer. There were one or two fish moving on the far side of the pool, but they were rather further across than she could cast, so when she had finished covering the pool I took her down to fish the part of Greenbank that she could cover in her thigh waders and started at the top of Polwick myself. Normally I would have made a change in my fly but I was determined to prove the ghillie wrong as I had faith in the long-haired flies, even in summer conditions.

Sure enough, half-way down the pool I got a good pull and on striking was fast into a fish on the Tadpole. After I had landed my fish we changed pools as I knew that I could cover Greenbank properly in my breast waders, and sure enough, half-way down, I caught first a nice sea trout of around two pounds and then a good salmon, both fish on my dropper. These proved to be the only fish on the bank at lunchtime although my host and his wife had had several pulls.

After lunch I was told to fish the March pool from the left bank. This is another long, wide pool with a wide, fast stream at its head, broken by large boulders. This stream flows for about half the pool and then quietens down to a wide smooth tail. It is difficult wading from the left-hand bank as there are deep troughs between the large boulders, and great care and a wading stick are both essential. Fishing it for the first time is certainly a fairly hazardous operation.

I started at the top of the pool, casting as long a line as I could manage with comfort, and when I had covered the first twenty yards I saw a fish head and tail about ten yards below my fly. As I reached that spot I felt a stong pull, and a good fish set off downstream. At this point I was faced with two difficulties. The first one was getting to the bank, the second, assuming that I could manage the first and play my fish out, was landing the fish as I had no net or gaff with me and there was no suitable beaching place down the length of the pool. In practice all went well and I was able to find a small inlet in the steepish bank where I could just beach the fish. The only thing I had to be careful of was catching the dropper on the bank. However all was accomplished, and the fish landed which weighed just under twenty pounds. It is worth noting when you hook a fish while wading deep in a fast and rough stream, that it pays not to be in too much of a hurry to get ashore. If you keep a steady strain on your fish you can quite often settle it down and gradually get to the bank at your own pace. I have seen some anglers even turn their backs on the fish as they wade ashore. Don't be in too much of a hurry, for if you are it can well lead to a fall and a ducking which can shake the fish off. Also when you have to land a fish by yourself, especially if the fish is a large one, don't hurry too much. Even in pools like this one with steep banks and no shingle there will be small inlets where a fish can be beached and the important thing is to make sure that you have the fish played to exhaustion before you bring it ashore. Go a bit above the place you have chosen and shorten your line and swing the fish into the bank in one easy movement.

That was my only excitement of that afternoon and when we met at the hut I found that my host had caught a grilse in Greenbank. In the evening we decided to fish for sea trout and between us we caught six, of which I caught two, and I was lucky enough also to catch a grilse in Polwick, again on the unpopular Tadpole.

The next morning Jennifer and I had to leave at lunchtime as I had to be back at Rosehall for a meeting that evening, and I was sent to fish the March pool again. This time I found the wading slightly less difficult and was helped in this by blinks of sunlight which helped me to see the bottom. Several fish were showing and conditions looked perfect but I had no offer until I reached the tail, when a fish rose gently to the fly without touching it.

I then came ashore and decided to change the tail fly. Contrary to accepted wisdom I tied on a bigger long-haired fly, a Collie Dog with a silver body one and a half inches long. Again I went down to the pool, and this time was able to wade slightly deeper which enabled me to cover more of the pool and present my fly at a rather better angle. However nothing came to my fly until I reached the place where I had moved the fish first time down. This time there was a long pull, and striking firmly I found myself hooked into a wild fish. As I waded ashore I pulled off line to give the fish slack, as the fish had run off so fast that half my backing was out. As happens so often this worked, the fish turned, and in due course I beached a beautiful ten pound fish covered with sea lice.

When I returned to the fishing hut with my fish I found that my host's wife had caught a lovely fresh fish of seven pounds which made the total seven salmon and seven trout between us for the thirty-six hours that we had been fishing. Of course, in a sense I had been lucky to have caught as many as I did, but the point I am making is not a mere repetition of my own fortune but to show that you will catch more fish if you listen and are prepared to learn.

In this instance on the Spey the ghillie had not seen flies as large as the ones I was fishing with used in the summer. Instead of keeping quiet about them he held them up to ridicule. For myself, not only did I have faith in them but I knew that many of the fish in the river had been there for some time, there had been very few fish caught in the days just before our visit in spite of reasonably favourable water conditions, and the best chance was probably to show the fish a different type of fly to the ones they had been used to seeing. I could have been wrong, but in practice my flies were successful, and I proved my point. Indeed, as I was leaving, the ghillie came and asked for copies of the flies I had been using and he now uses them on that beat where they account for a large number of the fish caught there annually. But if I had not had the confidence to persevere with them I doubt whether I would have caught more than one, or at the most two, fish. A less experienced fisherman could easily have had his confidence broken by the ghillie's remarks and attitude and therefore have been persuaded to discard his choice of flies. This would have been a pity as the catch of the beat for that thirty-six hours would have been four fewer fish, and the effectiveness of these larger sized, long-haired flies would have remained unknown to the beat for sometime to come. Surely the lesson to be learnt from this incident is never, no matter how experienced you are, pronounce judgement on the effectiveness of a fly, however ludicrous it would appear to be until you have given it a chance to earn its own reputation.

An Open Mind

One of the things that I do firmly believe about salmon fishing is that there is always something new to learn. However experienced you are, and however well you know a river or beat, I would urge on you the attitude of the old stalker who at the end of his life was heard to say 'Every time I go to the hill those stags teach me a new lesson'.

In practice I think that most fishermen are prepared to experiment with the flies they use and to change size and patterns to suit the occasion. But often fishermen grow careless and neglect the one thing that does change more than anything else. This is the shape and conformation of the river. On the Cassley I deliberately set out to re-learn the river each year. Although I know it well, very often the winter floods have made some change to the river bed, shifting one important boulder in a pool or washing some gravel into the best lie so that a pool can alter, in so far as its taking productivity is concerned, unnoticed and overnight. Very often a pool can earn for itself a reputation as being worthless, and as a result it may almost never get fished, and the productivity of the beat suffers greatly as a result.

I remember an incident that happened to me many years ago which illustrates this point perfectly. I had been asked to fish the Gledfield water of the Carron one day in late April. As chance would have it I had never fished this water before but had fished the beat below on many occasions. When I got to the water my host met me and apologised that his keeper was not there to attend to me but explained that, the man had been up all night at a fox's den and would join me later in the morning. My host took me up to the top of the beat and left me to work my way down. On the way up he had warned me that the Little Falls pool which we had passed was too high to be worth fishing.

I duly fished the March pool at the top of the beat and then MacGregor, Gledfield and Raven's Rock on the way down but all to no avail, although conditions looked perfect. When I reached the next pool I noticed that it was a deep, swirly pool on a bend with little current running through it, but as I had not been told I could not fish it I thought that I had better try. To start with I tried fishing at the head which fished well, but in the middle of the pool the undertow dragged my fly down and the back water made this part almost impossible to fish down, so I decided to back it up. After about ten casts I hooked and landed a nice fish and then almost immediately hooked and landed two more and hooked another.

As I was playing this last fish I heard the keeper's voice behind me and after he had tailed my fish I turned to him and said that this seemed to be a good pool. At that he smiled and said that this was the first fish he had seen killed there for ten years and normally they never even bothered to fish it. When I told him it was my fourth he was, as you can imagine, quite flabbergasted. After that the Whirl pool, an apt enough name, became one of the best on the beat.

Another thing which I do conscientiously and which I urge on all anglers however experienced they may be, is to listen to everything that anyone may say on fishing, especially to any hints on how to catch fish and I never, never regard anything as rubbish until I have had a chance to prove or disprove it myself. I find it a rare day when I don't learn something when I am on the river bank and generally I learn from the ghillie I am with. I always make a point of trying to draw out from all the ghillies all the information that I can and I only wish there was some way of encapsulating all the available information and codifying it before it passes away.

Fashions in flies and tackle and presentation are changing all the time, and many of these changes in flies and tackle enable the modern angler to catch more fish more easily than their forefathers dreamed of. When someone comes to fish with me on the Cassley I always let them choose their own flies and tackle unless they specifically ask for advice. That way, however strange their choice may appear, I can get a lesson for nothing, for either it will be successful in which case I have learnt something new, or it won't and then I hope they will ask for advice. And the same thing applies to the manner in which people fish. It is perfectly possible for someone to adopt an unusual but effective way of covering the water, in which case I have again learnt something new, but if they miss out all the best taking lies in a pool then I will give them advice which I hope they will take.

I have learnt many things in this way and I will end this chapter with two instances, both of which have in their time brought me a number of fish that but for observation and patience I would never have caught.

Many years ago an Air Force Officer came to fish with us on the Welsh Dee. It happened that I had to go to Chester that day but I took him down to the river in the morning and showed him the pools to fish. One of these was called the Major pool, and was long and wooded with a short, wide neck. This pool was peculiar in that the neck deepened suddenly behind a large submerged rock and then it flowed gently along beside a smooth rock ledge which ran out from the right-hand bank for seventy or eighty feet. The ledge started forty feet below the large rock and at the bottom extended some thirty feet out into the pool. At low water you could walk along this ledge in shoes and we generally fished this part of the pool from it with a minnow or prawn, although it did fish better from the other bank with bait.

It was a fact that we could catch fish in the pool on a fly in the neck at the top but even though we could reach the part of the pool below the submerged rock, and even though many fish rested there, we very seldom caught any fish on a fly in that part of the pool although the minnow and prawn accounted for a good number. The Air Force Officer was a fly fishing purist and as it was May he was fishing with a greased line and small flies.

I returned to the river late in the afternoon and stopped the car above the Major pool to see whether I could see him. To my amazement he was standing on the ledge casting upstream and across towards the submerged rock, and I could see that he was retrieving his line fairly quickly. I must confess that my first thought was that he was snatching, so I worked my way quietly through the wood above the pool to where I could see what he was doing.

He had no idea he was being watched but kept on casting away, varying the angle of his cast, sometimes more upstream and some-times more across, now retrieving a bit faster and now slower, his line all the time being clearly visible on the slow smooth surface of the pool. After about a quarter of an hour I saw a fish make a head and tail rise and then his rod bent as he hooked it. At this point I left the wood and helped him land a lovely twenty-one pound salmon which was hooked firmly in the scissors on a No. 10 Lady Caroline.

I was fascinated by this method of fishing and asked him how he had fared. He said that he had seen a number of fish higher up but had had no success until he reached the Major pool. There he had tried the fish from the usual stance on the field above but none would move to his fly, so he thought he would try them from the ledge as this was a tactic which did work in pools of this nature. Then he calmly pointed to two more fish he had caught standing on the ledge.

After that I often tried his tactic from the ledge on the Major pool and caught many fish there on the fly. It is a technique that works in other pools and for anyone who wants to try it I will summarise the main requirements. It works best in a deepish pool holding a number of fish with a slow current. It helps if there is an upstream wind to ruffle the surface of the water, and you should cast across, or across and up, and strip in the fly to make it work down and across the stream. Fish that come to the fly commonly make a head and tail rise towards the centre of the stream and they are usually well hooked in the scissors. I am a firm believer in striking when I move or feel all my fish and in cases such as this I count firmly one, two before raising my rod.

The last method I am going to mention I thought for a time was a unique discovery, and was certainly amazed when I first saw it used but recently I read a good description of it in Patrick Chalmer's book *Where the Spring Salmon Run*. One day I came across an angler fishing a fast, narrow run. He had perched himself on a rock about three yards above the top of the run, and apart from a couple of casts to start off with he fished the whole of the thirty yards of the run without casting again, and without once removing his fly from the water. His method was to pull off a yard or so of line from his reel at a time and then work his fly back and forwards across the run with the tip of his rod. It reminded me of harling but there is no doubt that he covered all the water most thoroughly and was in complete command of his fly all the time. Although on the first occasion that I saw this the angler was unsuccessful, I have often seen him take a fish in this place in this manner and I would recommend it as well worth trying if there is a suitable pool on your beat. Chalmers, who had that marvellous gift for imparting his knowledge so lightly, said that it was best to use this method of fishing with a greased line in high summer when the river was very low as it meant that you disturbed the water less. I cannot argue with that.

The Buck Run on the river Oykel, upstream of the Washer-woman Falls, is another place where I have seen this method used with effect by the present ghillie George Ross's father, a most knowledgeable and wily hand at all methods of fly fishing.

Droppers and Dibbling

Whenever the water temperature rises above 48°F and the sunk lines and large flies of early spring give way to lighter tackle, I start fishing with a dropper. This is not a practice followed by many but I think it has a number of advantages and few disadvantages. I believe that more fish would be caught and the number of blank days would be fewer if more anglers were to adopt this habit.

I started fishing for salmon with a dropper when I was a boy. Like many children I was brought up as a wet fly fisherman and I used the traditional cast of three flies on the hill lochs of Sutherland and in the Kyle for sea trout. It puzzled me then that no-one ever appeared to fish for salmon either on the Welsh Dee or the Cassley, with more than one fly on their cast.

'Why,' I asked, 'does everybody fish quite happily for trout with three flies, but only one for salmon when salmon tackle is so much stronger?'

I never received an answer which satisfied me, and my puzzlement increased when I caught two salmon while fishing on the Kyle for sea trout with three flies. The first took a Grouse and Claret in the middle position and the second a Black Pennel in the bob position, and both fish were netted without any undue difficulty. Would I have caught these fish I wondered if I had only been fishing with one fly?

I decided therefore to try a dropper for salmon and I started one May in the face of strong parental disapproval, echoed by Menzies, my father's ghillie. Both upbraided me for wasting time and fore-told disaster in the shape of tangled casts, snagged and broken fish, with no ensuing benefit. In practice all went well and I can still remember the first fish I hooked on the dropper in the Lower Platform pool of the Cassley, coming to the net with the tail fly neatly looped round the cast out of harm's way. Indeed so successful did the dropper prove to be that both my father and Menzies took to fishing with one.

Let me summarise its main advantages. First of all it can be compared with shooting with a double-barrelled rather than a single-barrelled shotgun. It gives the salmon two choices of fly in one fishing and thus doubles your chance of catching a fish. Secondly it helps any fisherman to find the correct size of fly in half the time, and I firmly believe that the correct size is far, far more important than any choice of pattern. Thirdly the dropper is presented to the fish in a different manner to the tail fly. It usually fishes just that bit higher in the water and, being anchored by the tail fly, it is more stable, less subject to the whims and eddies of the current. I believe there are days when the precise depth at which the fly fishes can make an enormous difference to the bag.

The other great advantage of fishing with a dropper is that it enables the fisherman to 'dibble' his fly on the surface of the water. This is akin to the technique of the loch fisher, fishing in the old-fashioned Scottish style tripping the bob fly along the surface of the waves. When I was a boy I was taught to fish lochs in this manner and still do when I fish the lochs both for brown and sea trout. I think that it translates ideally to salmon rivers, particularly in the summer months when the water temperatures are high and the rivers are low. Again I think that more salmon would be caught were more fishermen prepared to experiment with this method of fishing. It works best when you can get close to the water and then, keeping control of the fly, let the dropper just brush the surface of the stream and flit from ripple to ripple. You should not get so close to the stream that you run the risk of disturbing the fish, but cast across the river, a longish rod is a help here, and then bring the dropper to the surface by raising the tip of the rod. It pays to work your way very slowly down a run when dibbling. Cast two or three times from each position and vary the manner and pace at which you bring the flies across the stream. Always let your flies hang in the current beside any ripple or swirl which would mean an underwater lie or possible taking place. Very often you will find that you can move a large number of fish when you are doing this and even though you won't hook all of them by any means, you can have a lot of sport when the normal methods fail you. Fish which come to the dibbled fly take it in three ways. They either suck the fly quietly off the surface, or they head and tail over it, or they come to it with a great splash and wallop, jumping on top of it. When they do this I feel that they are trying to drown the fly.

One of the excitements of dibbling is that you will always see the fish take, so you must beware of striking too soon before you feel the fish. Indeed it will pay you to lower the point of your rod or give some slack line as you see the fish come to the fly, otherwise you will find that you prick more fish than you hook. It is very, very difficult to prevent yourself giving an involuntary twitch when a fish really splashes at the fly but I comfort myself with the thought that fish that behave like this will either have aimed accurately and be hooked willy-nilly or miss altogether.

Of course dibbling is much more suited to the smaller rivers that you find in the north of Scotland than the larger east coast rivers. It is a method used particularly on the Helmsdale, but you will find runs and pots on all rivers where dibbling can be used and I recommend it to all fishermen.

When I fish with a dropper I always have a dropper length no longer that two and a half to three inches. If it is any longer than this it will tend to become entangled with your main leader. I make the dropper by cutting the leader and then joining the two parts with a blood knot, leaving one end sticking out at right angles to the cast itself. An alternative is to make a loop in the cast, using the knot which you use to attach the cast to the line, and then tie a short piece of nylon on to the loop. Whichever method you adopt it is a mistake to have the dropper and the tail fly too far apart. On a nine foot cast I have my dropper four feet above the tail fly and this allows me one foot of cast to waste changing the tail fly before I have to renew my cast. If you have the flies any further apart then you lose the stabilising effect of the tail fly.

As to flies I mount a No. 9 blonde Hairy Mary or Silver Stoat's Tail in the dropper position whatever the height of the water. I then ring the changes on the tail fly. Also I prefer double-hooked flies for the dropper. I find that tubes or Esmond Drury flies do get tangled up in the leader although a number of people swear by them, and I think that double-hooked flies hold the water better than single-hooked. They are definitely better when you are dibbling.

There is another dibbling tactic which you should try if the conventional small, double-hooked fly is not producing any results. Mount a large light tube in the tail fly position, one as long as two and a half to three inches and then fish this half in and half out of the water. Very often this can be successful when the fish have worked their way up into the fast running streams at the throat of a pool. Finally if you are dibbling with two flies fish a fairly heavy fly in the tail position as this helps to anchor the dropper better.

Of course when there is water and the river is running at a good level you should then forget about the dropper and fish as normal just as if you had one fly on your cast. The only thing to watch out for is the sign of a fish moving to the dropper, slightly nearer to you than you would expect.

Many people, I know, will not use a dropper because they are afraid that it will snag on the bottom when playing a fish, or on the bank when they are landing a fish, and that a fish will be lost as a result. I admit this can happen but in my experience it happens but rarely. I can only remember two occasions when this has happened to me. You must take more care when you are playing your fish, especially if it is hooked on the tail fly. I always try and get opposite to the fish and then hold it as high in the water as possible. If the fish is hooked on the dropper, nine times out of ten the tail fly loops up and hooks on to the cast above the dropper and out of harm's way. The main disadvantage of the dropper comes when you are fishing in a very high wind when you may find that the dropper causes a number of tangles. In these circumstances it may be easier to abandon it. Try shortening the dropper leg to start with but if that doesn't work cut it off. The other important thing to remember is to make sure that the person landing your fish, assuming that you are fishing with someone else, knows that you are fishing with a dropper. If they do not, then the spare fly can get caught in their clothing as they advance with the net and this will inevitably result in tears and tribulations.

I think the worst danger when fishing with a dropper is for a second fish to take the trailing fly while the first fish is being played. This has happened to me five times. Three times the second fish attached itself early in the fight and I was promptly broken, the other two times I hooked the second fish as the first was almost played out and both fish were landed.

Now if my words have so far failed to convince you that droppers in the summer are a good idea I will tell you a story of a day's fishing, and I swear that everything is absolutely true, although like all the best fisherman's tales it is a pretty tall story.

Many years ago I went to fish the Oykel in July at the height of the grilse run. In those days the Oykel was owned by Lady Ross of Balnagown and that July the hotel had no tenants and the fishing was being let by the day. The late George Ross, then the head ghillie, arranged to telephone me when the river was in order so that I could book a day through the manager of the hotel. In due course the rains arrived and after two days downpour George rang to suggest that I booked a rod on the top beat the following day. This I did.

When I arrived at the hotel the next morning my rod was mounted and I had a No. 7 Silver Grey in the tail fly position and a No. 9 Hairy Mary on my dropper. George Ross, who was to be my ghillie, was well known to me as he had been one of my many tutors when I was a boy. He queried my decision to fish with a dropper as the river was high, and also my choice of flies for the same reason. I knew, however, he was a great supporter of the dibble dropper, a technique he had learned from Major Gilroy, a tenant. We were fishing the top beat which was very rocky, and there were a great number of fish about. He stopped short of saying that the dropper would be more trouble than it was worth but I could see that was what he meant. When I told him I was determined to persevere he then argued that I would do better to change the position of my flies and to fish the larger fly in the dropper position. I said, no, I wasn't going to do that. I was just going to fish the two flies in the ordinary way as the river was too high to make any sort of dibbling a profitable occupation.

With that we agreed to differ and started fishing at the tail of the Falls pool. This was too high, so we moved on to the Crag pool. The neck was on the high side but half-way down I got a good pull just below the big rock which was under water. When landed this fish proved to be fourteen pounds, rather larger than I had expected and it was hooked on the dropper. I then fished down the pool again and moved a fish to the dropper straight away. This fish would not come again but as I reached the tail of the pool I caught a second fish, right on the lip, a tiny grilse only four pounds in weight, hooked like the first fish on the dropper.

We then moved on to the George pool, in those days a superb taking pool which could often produce several fish when it was in order. We started just below the head of the pool as that part was too high and almost first cast a fish took me just on the near side of the stream. After a brief fight this too was in the net, a model grilse of five pounds smothered with sea lice, and once again hooked on the Hairy Mary dropper. Then just where the pool widens out I caught a second fish, and a third at the tail, both salmon, neither absolutely fresh and both hooked on the dropper.

44

Fir Pool – River Oykel.
A typical rock pool.

As we finished fishing the George pool George Ross suggested that we should change the tail fly and replace it with a shrimp, but the change made no difference as the last fish of the morning came from the Washerwoman pool, a nice fresh grilse of six pounds which played like a sea trout mostly out of the water, the sixth fish to the Hairy Mary that morning. As well as the fish I had caught I had moved another three fish and would swear they had all come to the dropper which meant that I had not, to my knowledge, had a single offer to my tail fly all morning.

As we lunched George and I discussed, in the time-honoured manner of fishermen, this extraordinary occurrence. I felt that there was a crucial difference in the way that the flies were fishing, but George felt that it was just one of those days when the fish only wanted one pattern of fly which happened to be the Hairy Mary I was fishing with in the dropper position.

To settle the matter I offered him my fly box and asked him to select a replica of the Hairy Mary I was fishing with and to tie it in the tail position so that I would be fishing with two identical flies. While he was doing this I jokingly predicted that it wouldn't make the slightest difference and that all the fish I caught that afternoon would be caught on the dropper. I don't suppose that either of us really believed that would be the case but in practice that is precisely how things turned out. That afternoon I caught another six fish and lost a further four, the last of which, at the end of the day, broke my cast and departed with my lucky fly. Two fish came from the Flat pool, three from the George and the last of the day from the Einaig Falls pool. This all took place before five o'clock when I stopped fishing as I had a business appointment at Rosehall at five thirty p.m.

What lessons can be drawn from the extraordinary day? Certainly every fish I landed, and I would swear every fish I hooked or moved, took the dropper. On the face of it had I not been fishing with a dropper I might well have had a blank day, and this was on one of the the best grilse rivers in Scotland, at the height of the grilse run with the river in absolutely perfect order and full of fish.

I think that there are days when salmon are attracted to a fly if it is fished in a particular way. That day I conclude they wanted a fly fished right in the surface film, and therefore they took the dropper in preference to the tail fly as it was closer to the surface and also held steadier in the high water. All that day I fished both flies in the normal manner and I never attempted to dibble the dropper or fluff it along the surface.

If you do this regularly you will find that on some days you will catch nearly all your fish on the dropper and on others the tail fly will claim the majority of the bag. Very seldom will it be divided equally between the two. I know several fishermen who would agree with me on this. I conclude from this that there are days and certain temperatures when the depth at which the fly fishes makes a crucial difference to the bag and it is this, rather than anything else which makes fishing with the dropper so successful.

I know some scoffers who say that any fish caught on the dropper has moved to the tail fly first. There is no doubt that this can and does happen. But I have spent many hours watching fish taking from the vantage points of high gorges above the river and I can say with absolute certainty that this is the exception rather than the rule.

Greased Line Fishing

It is surprising, perhaps, that this term has survived into the 1980s as today, with modern fly lines, grease is virtually a thing of the past. But survive it has, and with it have also survived the misconceptions that have dogged this method of fishing ever since it was invented by Arthur Wood of Cairnton on Dee in the 1930s.

There is a book by Jock Scott called *Greased Line Fishing for Salmon* which outlines Wood's methods. However, I do not think that anyone who wishes to learn the real reasons for greased line fishing will, in fact, learn very much from this book. Jock Scott in a way failed to grasp what Wood was doing, and his explanations are at times confused. Nevertheless the book does contain a great deal of Wood's advice on salmon fishing in general, much of which is invaluable.

The term 'greased line fishing' came about because in those days all fly lines were made of plaited silk. These Kingfisher lines had to be greased before they would float on the top of the water and as Wood's methods required a floating line, the term became synonymous with fishing with a greased line which floated on the pool. Many anglers who fish in the summer grease their lines in any case as this reduces the amount of effort required for casting. But greased line fishing is really a different thing and to explain it properly I must examine briefly the varieties of flies that an angler would use during the course of the year.

There is no doubt that the larger flies, particularly those used in the spring, were primarily dressed to imitate small fish of different sizes and varieties. In the old standard patterns of flies the Jungle Cock feathers which fly dressers placed on either side of the wing just behind the eye of the fly were put there for the specific purpose of imitating the eyes of a fish, and if fished correctly all these flies imitated fish of differing sizes as they traversed the width of the pool, quivering and darting as they were buffeted in the eddies and cross currents of the river.

In the summer the bright flies that were most successful in the spring gave way to duller coloured imitations and these were dressed to imitate waterborne invertebrates or other insects. There is little doubt that those fly dressers who invented the original patterns realised the importance of the details. Apart from fish and invertebrates, another of the main parts of a salmon's diet when at sea is plankton, a type of vegetation which literally hangs almost motionless in the water. Various types of plankton can also be imitated using dull coloured flies or the small dark varieties of the modern tube fly.

I firmly believe that if you are going to be a successful fisherman one of the first things you must do at the start of each day is to decide which of these creatures you have at the end of your line, and to simulate and imitate to the best of your ability the action of this lure as it swims through the water. If you decide that you have a small fish at the end of your line then you should allow it to come across the pool in the same way as a small fish would swim, letting it slow down and then dart quickly in small jerks. If the current of the pool is not sufficient to create the action then you must hand line to help your lure cut through the water in a natural manner. If you are imitating a waterborne invertebrate this should be fished more slowly, high in the water, with the occasional quick, jerky movement. And if you are imitating one of these it is probably best done on a greased or floating line in low water flows, although in high water you can use a slow sinker or a line with a sinking tip. However, if you decide that you wish to imitate plankton you must avoid all possible movement and drag on your line and let the lure hang in suspension in the current as motionless as you can contrive. It is therefore necessary for the angler to use a greased or floating line so that the fly is kept suspended high in the water, and this will also enable the fisherman to mend his line continually so that at all times it lies straight upstream of the lure and parallel to the current flow in the pool. This is the only way that any angler can prevent his line dragging or transmitting any movement to the fly.

Mending your line is not difficult and it only requires a small amount of practice for any angler to become proficient at it. As soon as your cast has landed on the water raise the rod and rod tip parallel to the water and make a controlled lift of the line up and across the stream. This slows down the movement of your lure across the river and if the flow of the current makes the line bag or kink then you can mend again to correct this. Sometimes an angler might have to mend his line up to half a dozen times before he has fished out the width of the pool.

I am absolutely positive that Wood based his method of greased line fishing entirely on the movement of plankton and this is the key to his undoubted success. There is no doubt that the greased line method of fishing, properly executed, does enable the angler to fish his fly right on the top of the water and I do think that this is a factor which quite often brings success.

I remember the first time that I came across the greased line technique as advocated by Wood. It was early one June during the war, on the Welsh Dee at a time when the river had been dropping slowly for over a fortnight and fresh fish were no longer able to run the river. There was however a good stock of fish in the main holding pools, but we had been killing fewer and fewer and during the last week had only caught one on the fly. A keen fishing friend of my father who had just been fishing the Aberdeenshire Dee came to stay for the weekend, full of enthusiasm about the greased line method as advocated by Wood. Although we told him that conditions for fly fishing were far from favourable this did not seem to put him off at all, but merely fired his enthusiasm rather than dampening it.

The next morning I took him down to the river and suggested that he should fish the Summer-house pool, but he made me fish it down first while he put up his rod and greased his line. I did as he wished and none of the fish showing in the stream at the head of the pool took any notice of my fly at all. When I had finished, my companion picked up his rod and line on which he had tied a No. 10 Lady Caroline and starting at the head of the pool he cast out over the stream and mended his line to allow the fly to hang in the current. In this part of the pool the stream bore in on the bank from where we were fishing, and the best taking lies were near the tail of the stream about fifty yards below the head of the pool. Just above my favourite taking place I saw a fish head and tail on the far side of the stream and moments later I saw my companion's rod bend as he hooked it. After seven or eight minutes he landed a well-shaped fourteen and a half pound salmon with his fly firmly embedded in the hinge of the jaws, and very kindly he urged me to take his rod and try this method of fishing. However I refused as I wanted to see exactly how he did it, and as he fished on at the very tail of the pool he hooked another fish which took a long time to land and weighed twenty-three pounds. After that, we went on down to the Major pool and in the next two hours I watched him fish this pool several times during which he caught another two fish weighing seventeen and fifteen pounds respectively.

In the next two days I landed a further five fish for him, making his total nine for a short three day stay with three fish weighing over twenty pounds. Although I fished the ordinary method fairly hard and fished much of the water in front of him I never moved a fish at all during this period, in spite of fishing with the same fly for a good deal of the time.

Ever since that time I have used this method successfully but I must admit that I prefer to use it as a sort of secret weapon when all else has failed, rather than a standard technique. I am often asked why, when it is so effective, I do not use it more and in truth I do not really know the answer to that except, I suppose, that I am a great believer in hand lining and keeping my fly moving even when fishing a floating line in the summer, and because I have such faith in this method I am reluctant to abandon it. However, if you are having a blank day in high summer when conditions look ideal and the fish are unaccountably stiff, it is the easiest of all alternative presentations to adopt as you need make no change at all to your tackle, merely change the way that you present the fly to the fish.

I think it is true on rivers like the Welsh Dee that when this method is likely to be most effective in April and May, the trees that line the heavily wooded bank burst into leaf and the bud sheafs then fall on to the surface of the water. This means that for days on end the use of small sizes of fly are not nearly so effective. Not only do the small flies fished near the surface continually catch the bud sheafs but I think the salmon themselves are lulled into a sense of complacency as they gaze up at many hundreds of small objects constantly passing above their heads. When this happens I have found that fishing with a floating line and small fly is virtually useless; and the same conditions can occur during leaf fall in autumn. On the rivers in the North where there are few deciduous trees on the banks then this time of the year, late April/May, can be the best time to fish with the greased line method, and the only thing I would urge on everyone is to fish your pool down first of all hand lining to imitate a small fish and then fish it down using the greased line method. I think that this procedure assures the fisherman that he is not bypassing a taking fish that might otherwise be in the bag.

My final comment on greased line fishing is that I do not think it is so successful a method these days as it used to be. The old Kingfisher lines when greased floated higher in the water than modern aircell floating lines; these lines were also easier to control and this makes that infinitesimal but vital difference to this type of fishing.

Bait Fishing – The Pros and the Cons

On the 14th March, 1950, I boarded the sleeper at Inverness to arrive at Crewe early the next morning. The salmon fishing season on the Welsh Dee opened then on the 15th March and I was bidden to my father's home, Argoed Hall, to fish the first two days of the season.

That year the river was low. Not unfishable, but low, and the weather was mild. There were a number of fish showing in the pools and we were hopeful that prospects would be good. My father had arranged for two rods to be set up, one was mounted with a 1/0 Yellow Torrish which he fished with, while mine had a 2/0 Silver Wilkinson on the cast. Both these flies were early season favourites on our piece of water.

We reached the river soon after seven o'clock in the morning, and as my father had to leave for work soon after eight thirty I persuaded him to start at the top of the Summer-house pool as this presented the best chance of a fish. I went to fish the New pool just above. This was a small, deep run which usually only held three or four fish at a time and was fished from a wooden platform projecting out over the water. This enabled the angler to cover the water, as otherwise the pool would have been unfishable since it was bordered by trees which made casting impossible. As I walked on to the platform I looked down river, and to my delight saw that my father's rod was already bent. He was attended by Joe Jones, the handyman, so there was no need for me to move and I started casting. First cast, however, I caught the trees behind me and as I returned to the platform having untangled my fly I looked and saw a straight rod and two dejected people examining the fly that had come free.

I then applied myself to my task and straight away I got a long pull and was into a fish. As I glanced down river to see whether I could expect any help I saw that my father's rod was bent for a second time and knew that I would have to fend for myself. There is always, I think, a particular tension about landing the first fish of the season. However long you have fished and however many salmon you have caught you are always anxious over your first fish. I know that I am, anyway. This fish was no exception, especially as it was no easy task to play and land a fish by yourself in the New pool. To start with I had to remove myself from the wooden platform which involved passing my rod around an iron stanchion, and I then had to slide down the steep bank to the water level. All went well however, and eventually I was able to beach a lovely spring fish on the stones by my feet. Just as I had killed my fish and tossed it up the bank on to the path, Joe arrived to help me with the sad news that my father had lost his second fish just as it was coming to the net.

We both walked downstream and as we reached my father his rod bent again and this time, I am glad to say, was third time lucky. My father then had to leave to go to his office and I decided to fish down the Summer-house pool again and after that leave it quiet for the rest of the day so that my father could fish it fresh on his return. I got no response at the 'diving stone' lie where my father had finished, nor to my surprise at the 'diamond stone' lie. The rest of the pool was really too still at that height of water but as it was the opening day I decided to fish on down to the lone tree. I changed my fly to one a size smaller because of the lack of current, and just above the lone tree I saw the wake of a salmon following my fly across the stream and then I felt a gentle pull as it took. This proved to be a smaller fish than the first two at nine pounds, and when I had landed it I decided to go straight down to the Major pool which I wanted to fish before the sun got too bright. This was a great big holding pool but the only part which was suitable for fly fishing was the run at the head of the pool, a wide run about twenty-five yards long.

I fished this run down twice with different sizes of fly but although I saw two fish move nothing came to my flies. I then went back to the run between the Summer-house and Major pools, intending to fish the remainder of the morning there. This pool required the longest casting of all the pools on the Argoed water as the main lie was across on the far side of the river and in addition was under a large oak branch which hung out over the water. To be successful the angler had to angle his cast under this branch to land as close to the far bank as possible, as only then would the fly fish the lie correctly. Many times in adverse wind conditions the angler would see his cast blown off course at the last minute. This day a fish moved in the lie just as I started fishing and when I covered the lie it moved to my fly without taking hold. I tried it with several other flies with no success but the spirit of perseverance was on me that day and I finally tied on a long-tailed yellow fly which Dr Hampson, a frequent guest at Argoed, used to use with considerable effect at times when the fish were difficult to catch. This fly did the trick and after a brisk struggle this fish, a beautiful thick set specimen weighing just over thirteen pounds was duly netted out.

After lunch I fished the Run and the Major pool again without success, although I saw a number of fish show in both places. I then went up and tried the New pool again and finally the Willow pool above it. This pool was a very small 'pot' which lay in the middle of the rapids below the Pentre, the big holding pool at the top of our water. To fish the Willow pool you had to wade two-thirds of the way across the river, as it lay under the far bank which was completely protected by trees and could not be fished from there. When I reached the vantage point from where I wanted to fish the pool I thought that it looked very low and clear, but as I had struggled over I thought that I had better give it a cast or two. To my surprise right at the tail of the pool I hooked a fish. This fish fought quietly to start with but then decided to return to the Summer-house pool below. It was impossible to follow at any pace as I was stuck in the middle of the river, so I gave the fish as much line as possible and struggled ashore as best I could through the boulder-strewn rapids. Luckily the fish stopped above the New pool and I was able to get opposite it. I knew that if it went down any further I would not be able to follow it so I decided to give it no line at all and trust to the hookhold and the strength of my cast. Fortunately this worked. And, in parenthesis, I would say that there are occasions playing a fish when you have to adopt these tactics. Thank goodness not very often, but when you do decide to reel the fish ashore you just have to reel and hope for the best.

This was my fourth fish of the day and the last, for my father had no luck in the Summer-house pool on his return from work and when he had fished it down we decided to call it a day.

The next day my father had to catch the mid-day train to London so we decided to get up early again and he would fish until eleven a.m. when he had to leave for the station. We decided that he would fish all the fly water while I would fish the Pentre and the lower parts of the Major pool with a minnow and bait as these pools were too still, at that height of water, to fish in any way with the fly. This we did.

My father caught a fifteen and a half pound fish in the New pool and then a twenty-two pound beauty in the Summer-house pool, both on the Yellow Torrish, his lucky fly. I fished the Pentre pool first with a black and orange minnow, then with a golden sprat and finally a spinning prawn. I killed two fish seventeen and eight pounds on the minnow and another of nineteen pounds on the spinning prawn. Just before lunch I caught another from the pulpit in the Summer-house pool on the floating prawn, and after a quick lunch I went down to the Major pool where I caught another three fish, one of nine pounds from the neck of the pool on a floating prawn, the other two weighing seventeen and seventeen and a half pounds from the still deep water, one on a sprat and the other on a spinning prawn.

That ended our successes and a marvellous two day's fishing. I had landed eleven fish altogether, using a variety of methods, while my father had caught another three in the short time that he had fished, all on the fly. The Welsh Dee was, in those days a marvellous river, and the high average weight of the spring fish, our catch averaged fourteen and a half pounds was an added thrill and excitement.

I must admit that I have enjoyed recalling those two days. They were a memorable fishing trip but the main purpose is not mere self-indulgence, but to provide some basis for discussing the different ways of fishing for salmon. There are many people I know who believe that all forms of bait fishing and spinning should be banned and that the only form of fishing that should be allowed is fly fishing. This is the case in the rivers of the north of Scotland where by proprietors' agreement nearly all the rivers north of, and including the Kyle of Sutherland district, are fly only throughout the season. The Tweed also is fly only from the 1st–14th February and from the 15th September until the 30th November, in other words those periods of fishing which fall outside the legal netting season from the 15th February–14th September. On other rivers, again by proprietors' agreement, spinning either stops on a predetermined date such as the 15th April or is prohibited when the river is running below a certain level. For myself I am not convinced that this works very well. In the olden days when rivers were generally fished by proprietors and their friends such a regulation was relatively easily enforced. Nowadays when nearly all beats are tenanted this is not so easy, and it is worth noting that only on the Tweed does this regulation have the force of law.

In the north of Scotland in the old days, and by this I mean before the last war, there was such a thing as 'fishing height'. When the river fell below a certain level the head ghillie would inform the proprietor that the river was below fishing height and all fishing would cease until it rose again. I did hear of one river where this regulation was enforced in 1983 but there is no doubt that it is tricky as most fishing is let many months ahead. Most tenants travel long distances to fish for their one week or fortnight of the year and I can imagine the reaction of a tenant of a costly beat arriving only to be told that he could not cast on the river as it was too low. Even worse perhaps if he (or she) was rung and told the river was too low to make travelling worthwhile on Friday, and then the rains arrive over the weekend and the river is in perfect fishing ply on the Monday. I think that such a ruling could well lead to compensation claims and possibly litigation.

The purpose and idea behind such a ban was, of course, to prevent the fish constantly being disturbed in the very low water. Well it is definitely possible to do this, but in my experience it is perfectly possible to catch a number of fish on a fly even in the lowest water conditions of high summer, and I know a number of accomplished anglers who would agree with me. I have written of summer fishing and how I would tackle it in my first book *Fly Fishing for Salmon* so I will not cover this subject in detail here. Suffice it to say that I think you should stand well back from the water and get up very early in the morning.

All this may seem a far cry from the arguments about bait fishing and spinning. However I will stick my neck out and say that in my opinion there are many rivers where spinning could and should be curtailed and that this would make very little difference to the overall catch of the water. I think that the reason why so much spinning is seen on rivers like the Aberdeenshire Dee which is ideal fly water is that people find it easier to cast a minnow, which it certainly is. They cover more water, which they certainly can and they believe that if they spin they will catch more fish. I think that if only the spinners took the trouble to learn to cast a fly adequately under any conditions then they would catch as many fish as they do at the moment. Let me present my case. And I will confine my arguments to the Tweed, as I know that if I quote the examples of the rivers of the north of Scotland which I know best, people will aver that these rivers are peculiarly suitable for fly fishing. Indeed they are, and I know no-one who fishes there who would admit to being handicapped in any way by the fly only rule.

Modern equipment, in particular the differing types of fly lines, floating, slow sinking, fast sinking, lead-core enable the angler to fish at a variety of depths. Similarly the powerful modern rods made from carbon and glass fibre enable the fisherman to cast a much heavier fly with relatively little effort. In this respect I think that the fly fisherman now has the advantage over the spinner who has to rely on the weight of the minnow, or the amount of lead he attaches to his line to achieve the depth he wants. The fly fisher can control the pace and angle of his fly far, far better than the spinner, and it is virtually impossible for the spinner to fish with a light lure of any sort as he would be unable to cast it far enough.

As I have said the Tweed is fly only after the 14th September until the end of the season on the 30th November. The autumn period is usually wet, the river is often high and discoloured. The Tweed is also a very wide river with many banks tree-lined and yet a very large number of fish are caught on the Tweed annually at that time of year, all on the fly. Admittedly a number are caught from boats which are necessary to reach and cover the lies properly, and this being the case I really wonder whether more rivers should not adopt the fly only rule for longer periods.

There is no doubt that when spinning is allowed throughout the year the fish do get disturbed when people spin in the low water of summer. Also if the river is at all rocky the bed of the river can get littered with snagged minnows and nylon line which is not only unsightly but it is a hazard when fish are being played and also dangerous for birds.

But I would counsel that this attitude does depend on the water that you are fishing. There are rivers, the lower reaches of the Wye, and a large number of pools such as the Pentre and Major pools on the Welsh Dee that I have written about where the annual catch would be drastically reduced were fly only the rule. Such pools and rivers are too slow flowing to allow the fly to work properly and also being tree-lined they are protected from the wind so that the surface of the water never gets ruffled in any way and there is never any chance that they can be fished by backing up. These waters have to be fished either by spinning or with a bait and it would be quite wrong to try to enforce any rule to the contrary.

Spinning is one thing. Bait fishing is quite another, and by bait fishing I mean prawn or shrimp, worm fishing of all kinds and the drop natural minnow. All these baits can be deadly on their day when they are fished properly. As in so much of salmon fishing, Chaytor sums up admirably the main *raison d'être* of fishing with the prawn, and for those who do not know the passage I will quote it in full.

'Being all (forty or fifty salmon) caught in hopeless fishing they took a great deal of fishing for, but still I am far from being an experienced prawn fisher. In truth I rather dislike fishing with prawn for several reasons. First of all, the fish have never played as well when hooked on the prawn as they did when taken on the fly, or even when taken on the minnow. I do not know the reason for this. Possibly to some extent it is because my prawning has been done in dead-low water when fish are apt to be less vigorous, but anyhow I am quite sure that the same fish would have fought much better on the fly.

Another reason for which I avoid much prawning is that it is a boring and messy business to bait the hooks, even with fresh prawns, and the preserved ones are just as messy, and generally have an offensive smell. Also I cannot think it quite fair and sportsmanlike, if one has guests or neighbours, to be constantly dragging great red prawns through the pools that they will have to fish with the fly the same day.

Still a good many times in *hopeless summer or autumn water*, I have got a good fish on the prawn...' (the italics are mine).

That really sums it up. In spite of all the reservations there are times when you will only catch a fish if you fish with a prawn or shrimp or possibly a worm, and in an ideal world if I knew that such methods of fishing were not going to be abused I would advocate bait fishing even on the fly only waters of the north of Scotland.

First of all every fisherman will have to admit that there is no way that the fly fisherman can attempt to imitate the natural bait. They stand, and smell, alone. Secondly when fish get stuck in a pool, generally in very low water, the only way they can be caught is on a natural bait and if they are not then the best lies in the pool are tenanted by stale, uncatchable fish which has a very detrimental effect on the productivity of the beat.

The main objection raised by the anti-bait fishermen to prawn fishing in particular is that it disturbs the water and fish are frightened out of the pool and rendered uncatchable. Possibly this can apply when the prawn is fished clumsily in very low water conditions but in my experience this happens very seldom. When we were boys my brothers and I used to fish with the prawn regularly on the Welsh Dee. Much of our water, as I have said, was only suitable for spinning and bait fishing but my father fished only with the fly at all times and in all heights of water. In the summer he would encourage us to fish the best fly water with a prawn before he returned from work in the evening and then he would go down and fish the same water through with a fly. Very often he would be successful with the fly even when we had fished the pool without result with a prawn just before, and Arthur Wood recounts exactly the same experience at Cairnton-on-Dee.

On many occasions I have sat in the wood at the tail of the Major pool and spent a whole afternoon swimming my prawn suspended on a float (and if the purists reading this are too horrified I would ask them to forgive the enthusiasms of youth) through rows of fish that I could clearly see lying in the shade beneath the cliff face. Although the prawn would literally bump along their noses all they did was quietly part ranks and let it pass through them. Never did any fish bolt at the sight of the prawn and I was in a perfect vantage point to see down into the water. Once the prawn had been swum through their ranks more than half a dozen times very seldom would one of these stationary fish take, but if by chance an outsider joined their ranks from some other part of the pool, then that was a different matter and it would not be uncommon to catch this fish shortly after.

Probably the most reviled bait of all is the garden worm but I think that the fisherman who can catch more than his share on the worm is probably the finest fisherman of all. The natural worm, allowed to ramble down the stream fished on a fly rod, causes the least offence and in my view the least disturbance to the water.

So there we have it. On the one hand I am a devout and devoted fly fisher and always will be. I think that far too many rivers permit bait fishing, particularly spinning when they shouldn't. On small rivers fly only should be the rule for the greater part of the salmon fishing season. On the other hand there are rivers where such a restriction would make no sense at all and baits of all kinds have to be used throughout the year otherwise no fish would be taken. And contrariwise I think that there are water conditions in the summer when fly fishing is fairly hopeless. Then it might be permissable for a tenant to use worm only on a fly rod and possibly only for the specified hours of the day.

Many years ago a friend of mine went to fish the Aberdeenshire Dee one June for a weekend. Heavy rain on Friday meant that the river was high and coloured and that Saturday morning my friend was told by his ghillie that he must fish with worm. He was a fly fishing purist and refused and caught the only fish of the day on a small blue and silver tube.

Bait Fishing Techniques

There is an old fishing poem about a worm which starts with 'and with this bait have often taken been the salmon fair of river fish the best', that was written nearly four hundred years ago, but it is a true statement and for the benefit of anyone who has not had experience of fishing for salmon with natural bait – prawn, shrimp, worm and natural minnows, I will describe how it should be done.

Prawn Fishing: There are four ways of fishing with the prawn, each of which can be very effective on their day. These are rambling or trotting, floating, sink and draw and finally spinning. The first three methods are normally used when the river is low but you can spin with a prawn very effectively when the river is high. Which method used must be up to you, but the character of the pool you are fishing does really determine which is the most effective.

To start with I will take the trotting or rambling prawn as this method is the most exciting and can be used either on a fly rod of between twelve and fourteen feet in length, or a spinning rod. I would recommend that a rod of over twelve foot in length is used as this does give the angler more control over the prawn as it rambles down the stream. First of all the prawn has to be mounted on an ordinary bait hook size 1–10 with a nylon or wire trace attached. The best prawns are good red ones and I prefer those with red eggs between their legs. Straighten out the prawn, attach the bait needle to the loop of the bait hook trace, and then thread the bait needle through the head of the prawn, pass it carefully along the fleshy back so that it comes out in the centre of the tail between the fins. When you have done this, draw the trace through the body until the bait hook is lodged securely in the head of the prawn. You then have to bind the body of the prawn securely to the shank of the bait hook. You should do this either with pink silk, or better still very light copper wire, because if this is not done then the body of the prawn will break up as you cast and as good, natural prawns are extremely expensive this is wasteful. When you bind the prawn to the bait hook be careful to place the bindings between each set of legs so that they stand out and are not compressed against the side of the prawn by the binding material. Some people prefer to use a long pin as well as the shank of the bait hook to make certain that the body of the prawn is straight when it is being fished, but I have always found that a long shanked bait hook is perfectly adequate.

When the prawn is mounted, and it is a good idea to mount two or three before you start fishing, attach the trace to your line with about four foot of nylon if you are fishing with a fly rod and fly reel, or, if you are fishing with a spinning rod, just tie the trace to the spinning line. Sometimes if you are fishing very fast flowing water it will pay you to have a small weight, preferably a spiral one attached about three feet up the line from the prawn. Start at the top of your pool about ten yards down from the head and then lob the prawn upstream into the neck of the current entering the pool. As the prawn comes floating down towards you raise the tip of your rod or draw in line so that you are always in immediate contact with the prawn and then, as the prawn floats pass, either release line or lower the rod tip to allow the prawn to move freely down the pool without dragging. Once the prawn has fished itself out and starts to drag then hand line in quietly and recast. In theory this method allows the prawn to swing and gyrate in the eddies of the current as it floats down the stream, stabilised by the weight of the prawn and/or the weight attached to the line which is positioned to give the prawn depth and to regulate its movement in the water. Always keep in constant touch with your prawn so that it does not snag on the bottom and you can only do this by hand lining or raising the tip of your rod. If a fish takes and the prawn stops then you must strike immediately, and if you have too much drowned line then you will obviously miss your fish.

There is no doubt that a long rod is extremely helpful when fishing the rambling or trotting prawn because it gives you more direct control. I also think that the weight of the fly line stabilises the movement of the prawn in the water far more effectively than the lighter monofilament mounted on the modern spinning reel.

Try four to six casts from each position and then move downstream three or four yards at a time, and repeat this until you have fished out the streamy part of the pool. Once you get to the deader part of the pool this method is really less effective but if you wish to continue into the slacker current then you should remove the weight if you are using one. Ideally this method works best in narrow, streamy pools or cambered pools where the current bears in strongly on one bank. It is also very effective in small pots and rocky pools but it does not work so well in a pool which has a wide broad head or in wide, slow moving pools. Any pool which has a high bank or one where you can stand a distance above the water is well suited to this method of fishing because this enables you to have a better control over your bait, but this is by no means essential and I have, on occasions, used the rambling or trotting prawn very effectively when I have been wading fairly deep at the head of a run. The head of the Summer-house pool on the Argoed side of the Welsh Dee was ideal for this type of fishing.

The Floating Prawn: This method is probably best suited to the older type of spinning rod of around ten to eleven feet in length but you can use a normal fly rod perfectly adequately. Mount the prawn in the same way as for the rambling or trotting prawn and attach a small weight about three feet up the line from the prawn. When you have done that, attach a large float about four to eight feet above the prawn, and this distance will vary according to the depth of the water that you are fishing.

It is an advantage to grease your line for about twenty yards between the float and the rod so that your line sits on the surface of the water and does not become drowned. This allows you to strike quickly if a fish takes, and it also stops the drowned line from drowning the float itself. Start at the top of the pool using the same tactics as you would fishing a rambling prawn, lobbing the prawn up into the head of the pool, and then as the prawn comes past you just let the line run off the reel and allow the float to carry it on down the pool. If it will, I let the prawn float down about twenty or thirty yards before checking it and then wind in very slowly. If you are fishing a wide pool start off by letting the float come down the near side of the pool first and then cast across the centre and then to the far side so that the prawn is shown to all the fish in the pool, regardless of where they are lying, over its entire width. When a salmon takes the prawn the float will begin to bob on the surface and may be pulled across the current or upstream, or even on occasions downstream. When this happens you should pay out a slack line and wait until the float is pulled

A wooded pool – River Eden.

below the surface of the water before striking, as otherwise you may pull the prawn out of the fish's mouth. I have often watched a salmon taking a floating prawn and very often when it does this it holds the prawn crossways in its mouth and plays with it before taking it properly. This is the time when the float begins to bob and move across the surface and therefore you should be patient and wait until the float actually plunges below the water before striking.

You should be careful to calculate the proper depth at which your prawn should fish as salmon rarely lie directly on the bottom of the pool and if your prawn is too deep you may actually be swimming it below where the fish are lying. To start with I would set my prawn at a depth of four feet, unless I knew the water well, and then gradually fish it deeper if I had no success at that depth. I would say, however, that it is rarely necessary to set your float higher than eight feet above the prawn and if you do, it is very difficult to cast any distance. A pool where there is a backwater, which the floated prawn can glide around in, can be a very effective taking place for this method of fishing.

Sink and Draw: When I have fished with this method I have always found it best to mount the prawn on an ordinary spinning mount with the spinning flight removed. Again, choose a good red prawn (preferably with red eggs between the legs), then straighten it out and insert the pin of the mount between the fins at the tail of the prawn and along the fleshy part of its back. Once the prawn is straight then the hooks of the mount can be placed carefully between the legs and underneath its head and then bound in position with either cotton or copper wire. The head of the prawn faces down the line and you should attach a good weight, preferably a spiral one, about four feet above the prawn on the line.

The sink and draw method works best, however, in a narrow deep pool, or a pool where the fish are lying in deep water beside a rocky ledge close to the bank, and it is not nearly so effective in shallower wide pools. Start fishing just above the deep water in the pool and stand about five yards above where the fish lie, and then cast across the pool square to the current. When your prawn hits the water keep your rod tipped low for about half a minute to allow the prawn time to sink, and then crisply raise the tip of your rod about six feet and then lower it again slowly. Continue this motion until your prawn has worked its way to the side of the pool at which time you should reel in and cast again. When you raise the tip of your rod you make the prawn shoot to the surface and it then falls slowly back into the depths of the pool dragged down by the weight. As it does this it gyrates gracefully in the eddies and currents. Fish which take the prawn fished in this way normally take it as it falls back into the depths or just as it begins to move once more to the surface. If you feel any pull or feel the prawn hesitate strike immediately, as fish are very inclined to snap at the prawn when it is fished in this way which is why it is mounted on treble hooks. This method can be extremely deadly when other techniques fail and I can only imagine that the salmon is attracted by the quick movement of the prawn as it is being drawn to the surface of the river as it reminds them of a small fish trying to escape.

It is an advantage to fish the sink and draw prawn with a fairly long rod and this is particularly true when the fish are lying against a rock ledge or a steep bank, as you can then hold the bait the correct distance across the river just beyond where the fish are lying without snagging the prawn on a ledge. You should pay particular attention to the distance that you place your weight above the prawn and this is just as important as the size of the weight that you use. The size of the weight must be governed by the strength of the current in the pool you are fishing. The closer you place the weight to the prawn the more you curtail the prawn's movement in the water as it drops back into the depths of the pool. I have often seen a fisherman be successful immediately he moves his weight a foot or so further away from the prawn. Always be prepared to experiment with this and very often the small adjustment can make the difference between success and failure.

That famous fisherman, the late Captain Hughes-Parry, used the sink and draw method of fishing a prawn with great effect on the Slaughterhouse pool of the Welsh Dee and this was a pool which was ideally suited to this method of fishing.

The Spinning Prawn: This is exactly the same as any other method of spinning and you do not need to adopt any special tactics. Mount your prawn with the head down the line on an ordinary sprat tackle inserting the pin between the fins of the tail and then sliding the tackle into place along the back of the prawn. This straightens out the body of the prawn and you then should bind the hooks of the tackle on to the body using copper wire or cotton. I have heard some fishermen say that the legs of the prawn should be bound against the body as this makes the bait more streamlined, but I personally believe in placing the binding between the legs so that they stand out even for this method of fishing. This does mean that the prawn wallows about in the water as it is being spun and I feel that this attracts fish and makes the bait more effective. This is rather akin to spinning for *Salmo ferox* or cannibal trout in lochs with a natural bait when you should place the flight in the shoulder of the small trout and not through its head to produce this wallowing motion. Use the spinning prawn in medium or low water or you can even use it in high water provided that the river is not too coloured. It is probably most effective in still wide pools or in the glide of the tail of a big pool. I used to use a spinning prawn on the Welsh Dee with great success from the opening day which in those days was 15th March until the end of May. Some of my friends used to use second quality prawns, that is, ones without eggs or those with black eggs, when they fished the spinning prawn but I would recommend that you use the best quality prawns available and do, if you can, use those with eggs between their legs.

I know that prawn fishing is a very controversial subject and many anglers believe that it should be banned. It is, however, a highly skilled method of fishing and, if it is *not abused*, it can be a useful addition to any angler's armoury as it often allows him to kill fish in stretches of water or parts of pools which would be impossible to fish in any other way unless he was spinning.

It is a fact that it very seldom pays to persevere with this bait. Fish either take it straightaway or completely disregard it and therefore a few casts with a prawn using the method best adapted to the particular pool you are fishing is quite sufficient to find out whether the fish are going to take the prawn that particular day or whether you should pack up and go home or resort to some other method of fishing.

I am sure that many people will be puzzled by the importance I attached to fishing with prawns which have eggs between their legs. When I started fishing as a boy I was always told by my tutors that you should use prawns with eggs and I was puzzled as to why this should be. Now after long experience, I am as convinced as they were of the importance of this and rightly or wrongly I put forward the theory that as the prawn is buffeted by the currents as it drifts down the river, these eggs are dislodged. They then float down in the water, and salmon scent them and often home in to the prawn by following the eggs to the prawn itself.

This theory may sound a bit far-fetched, but I am positive that it is correct. For example, in the wood on the right bank of the Major pool on the Welsh Dee there were two places ideally suited to fishing the floating prawn. One was immediately above a projecting buttress of rock close in to the bank and below this buttress was one of the main lies in the pool. No fisherman could work a prawn down to this lie because once it passed the buttress it was no longer within sight. This meant that you had to swim the prawn down above the rock buttress and then cast again when the float reached the projection. This was a section of the pool where fish seldom lay. However, when you fished this bit of the river with the floating prawn very often you caught a fish, and this usually occurred on the third or fourth cast. As there was a high bank above the river you could go and watch the fish lying in the main lie when the angler started fishing. Very often after one or two casts the fish in that lie become alert, and then moved up slightly in the water before swimming round the buttress and following a weaving course until they saw the prawn which they then took.

Another place was below the buttress at a small promontory we called 'Taylor's Stance'. From here we used to cast the prawn upstream and let it float down to the pool below where we stood. Here it got caught in the small backwater and the float circled around this little bay until we lifted the prawn up to cast again. Often I could watch fish following down the exact line that the prawn had taken just moments before turning in at the bottom of the backwater and gulping the prawn as they came back upstream. There is no doubt that in both these places the fish were following the scent that the prawn had left in the water as they could not possibly see it, and I firmly believe that this scent is provided by the eggs as they get washed out by the current. Certainly I have always found that a prawn without eggs was far less effective and I would go so far as to say that it is virtually useless, unless it is used for spinning in high water.

The Shrimp: Shrimp fishing is identical to fishing with a prawn in every detail and mounting the shrimp is exactly the same. It works best during the summer when the rivers are low and the temperature is high and the period from the beginning of May until the end of September is the best time. I have always found that the rambling and floating methods of fishing with shrimp are by far the most successful and on numerous occasions I have found that shrimp will work when the prawn has failed, although I would always believe in trying prawn first and never the other way about.

When rivers are low and the water temperatures are high, then bait fishers will find that they kill four fish on the shrimp to every one on the prawn, but here I am speaking of the natural prawn and in recent years those prawns dyed a deep purple in colour have proved very successful, particularly in the summer months. So successful have they become that the day of the shrimp may well be over.

Worm Fishing: Again, you can fish with the worm using the same methods as for prawn and shrimp except that you would not attempt to spin a worm. The main difference between worm fishing and fishing with prawn or shrimp is that when you feel a fish take you do not strike immediately, but pay out line to give the salmon time to swallow the bait before tightening. Very often you will feel a fish knocking at the worm for thirty seconds or even longer and when a fish is doing this he is rolling the worms around his jaws and occasionally may even let them go altogether before he takes them properly. This gentle, prolonged take is the really exciting part of fishing with a worm and gives this method of fishing its own particular thrill.

The main method of fishing with a worm is upstream, or rambling, and I think that it is best to use a single red worm on a single hook for this although you can, if you want, use a Stewart tackle. Cast the worm upstream in exactly the same way as for the rambling prawn, raise your rod tip as the worm floats down towards you and then lower it as the worm passes you and let it float away downstream. Always be careful to keep in contact with the worm so that you can stop either the worm or weight becoming snagged and always try to avoid dragging the worm as this is an unnatural movement. If a fish takes the worm will stop, and at this point you should start playing out the line for if a fish feels any drag or pull on the bait it will quite often spit the worm out, and then rarely return to it. If you wish you can attach a float as this will enable you to drift your worm right down the length of a pool. When a fish takes you will see the float starting to bob on the surface and again do not strike until the float has been pulled under the water.

When you are using the small, red dung worm it is an advantage to dig them a day or two before you plan to use them and then put them in a tin, with air holes, which contains a mixture of powdered red brick and soil. This helps to toughen the worms and they are less likely to break up when you cast. This is quite a good practice to follow with lob worms although these are less brittle than dung worms.

Some anglers use large lob worms to attract salmon and in this case two, or even three, are mounted on a No. 1 or a 1/0 bait hook and fished in exactly the same way as the small single worm. I do know that there are people who thread lob worms one after the other on the hook, but I have always found it best to embed the hook in the centre of each worm and allow both ends to trail down on either side. Either dead, low water conditions (even on a sunny day) or a rising river are my favourite times for using this bait. I have always been interested in this method of presenting lob worms as I do not believe that when the salmon was a parr there would have been many opportunities for feeding on this bait. I think that lob worms presented in this way simulate something that salmon feed on at sea, probably a member of the squid or octopus family.

The Natural Minnow: This is the last natural bait that can be used for salmon fishing and I think that it is best when fished with the sink and draw method. It is, of course, a well known bait to use for big wily old trout, but it can kill salmon that have become stale in pools after a prolonged spell of low water and it is worth trying, as a last resort, when all other baits have failed. Mount the minnow by passing a bait needle attached to a bait hook trace through the mouth of the minnow, down through the body, and out beside the tail. Fold a piece of lead or lead wire around the shank of the bait hook and then pull the bait hook into the mouth of the minnow so that the lead and shank lodge in its throat and the hook and barb lie outside its mouth against the gill casing. No further weighting up the line should be necessary.

Cast out the bait and work it in exactly the same way as you would a sink and draw prawn. Concentrate on those areas of the pool where the main lies are sited and also the necks of the pool and, surprisingly enough, if a fish takes do not strike immediately, but play out line in exactly the same way you would if you were worming. This allows the salmon plenty of time to gorge the bait and eventually you can strike crisply when you judge the time to be ripe.

All these methods of fishing with natural baits are not only very effective but also highly skilled. There is no doubt that a great deal of the art lies in the ability of the angler to mount and present the bait properly, and when you are fishing it is of the utmost importance to show the bait free of drag. There is, however, one proviso to this – salmon do sometimes take when you are reeling in to cast again. You should therefore always concentrate right up to the time when the bait leaves the water. The only other point I would make is that you should be careful not to handle the natural bait when your hands are covered with fly repellent as salmon have a very acute sense of smell and I think this is a mistake even when you are fishing with an artificial fly.

I have always been slightly perplexed why fishing with these natural baits, worm, shrimp and prawn are frowned upon when spinning with gold and silver sprats have always been accepted by most anglers without question. I cannot see any logical reason for such a differentiation and would say that of all baits, including all forms of spinning, the worm, fished properly, is the most harmless. It not only disturbs a pool the least but is the one bait which rarely, if ever, foul hooks a fish.

Tweed, late February 1940

I was convalescing at the time after a brief illness, and as my parents were going North to fish the Lower Floors water of the Tweed, they decided to take me with them. This was an annual event for them, as Sandy Prentice, a lifelong friend of theirs from Edinburgh, always asked them to fish as his guests. For me, it was my first visit to that wonderful river and naturally I was thrilled to have the chance to fish it. Normally I would have been sitting behind my desk in some dreary classroom at school.

We drove up from Wales in hard frosty conditions with snow on the roads as we crossed the high ground. As we crossed the Border the weather changed, and we arrived in Kelso just before dusk to a squally shower with a mixture of sleet and heavy rain. We were staying in the Ednam House Hotel overlooking the river and were met on our arrival by Mr Prentice with a forlorn expression on his face.

He had been there for a few days and sadly related to my parents that so far he had not even put up his rod as the river was almost entirely frozen over and quite unfishable. I will always remember the atmosphere at dinner that night in the dining room. Small groups of gloomy anglers huddled together at each table talking in monosyllables, and the blazing logs in the fireplace were certainly the most lively thing in the room. I was sent to bed early full of excitement at the thought of fishing the next day, and, being an eternal optimist, the fact that the river was frozen over and I would not, therefore, even get a cast probably hadn't sunk in. Tired after the long journey, I was soon sound asleep.

When I woke next morning, it was barely light. I lay in bed full of anticipation and was perplexed at the creaks and crunching noises which I could hear. I tiptoed to the window of my bedroom and peered out into the gloom. There was the river, a raging, brown torrent, carrying on its surface huge ice floes buffeted to and fro, crashing into each other as they were swept seawards. Here was the explanation of the strange noises I had heard from my bed.

At breakfast there was an entirely different atmosphere in the dining room, almost electric. Everyone anticipated what might happen later in the week when the river settled. Others, including ourselves, could hardly wait to get down to our respective beats and make up our rods. I will always remember driving through the grounds of Floors Castle that morning as we made our way to the river. The snowdrops and early daffodils seemed to have been released by the thaw and could be seen poking their heads through the vanishing snowdrifts. Spring, one felt, had really come at last.

When we arrived at the fishing hut besides the Ingham pool close to the bank of the river we were met by Veevers, the head boatman, and Oliver the second boatman. They helped us to unpack my father's shooting brake which was filled with every type of fly and spinning rod and all the equipment that was needed. They were both much relieved that the thaw had finally arrived because, as this was Monday morning, they knew very well that our chances of catching a fish later in the week were reasonably assured provided that the river settled.

That morning the river was literally bank high with ice floes, trees and other debris being washed past us as we watched mesmerised by the transformation that had occurred overnight. We mounted our spinning rods and put out our bottles of silver and golden sprats. These would be our first choice of bait once fishing started.

When we had finished unpacking, we drove into Kelso so that my parents could make their annual pilgrimage to Forrest Tacklemakers, where my father purchased his usual order of flies, casts, and minnows which he would need not only during the coming week but also for the whole of the season on the Welsh Dee and the Cassley at Rosehall.

As common sense and the years of discretion had not yet come to me I was extremely loathe to leave the river, and I fondly imagined that if I tried a cast or two I would catch a fish from under an ice floe. But I was under strict parental supervision, and biting my tongue I accompanied my parents to Forrest's shop where I gazed in astonishment at the wide variety of fishing equipment on display.

After lunch we returned to the river, hoping for a cast, but alas it was still rising and the boats were bobbing up and down like corks on the ocean wave as they were buffeted by the current even though they were well sheltered from the full force of the flow in their anchorages. There was nothing we could do, so reluctantly we returned to the hotel.

Unfortunately, it rained again that night and conditions had not improved on Tuesday. However, there was a touch of frost on Tuesday night and by the middle of the morning on Wednesday the river began to steady and hold. We tried all the the likely corners with large silver or golden sprats and a variety of weighty minnows but the river was still very high, and there was very little fishing except in the quiet corners close to the bank. About three thirty p.m. Sandy Prenctice killed a fresh run spring fish weighing seven and a half pounds on a golden sprat in the Ingham pool, but apart from that we never even moved a kelt.

Thursday was no better. The river was still very high and if anything, slightly more coloured than the previous day but towards evening it at last began to fall slightly more quickly. We had no luck, but the parties from the hotel fishing the other beats all had one or two fish between them. Friday dawned with a sharp touch of frost and as I peered out of my window I could see there was a considerable change in the height of the river. The rapids opposite were far less choppy and the islands in the water appreciably larger. I dressed quickly and met the others for breakfast, barely able to contain my excitement at the thought of fishing the Tweed when there was a real chance of catching a fish.

At the fishing hut both boatmen were obviously full of hope for the first time this week. All the rods had freshly mounted sprats on them and everything was prepared for a prompt start. My father went up to the Coach Wynd with Veevers, while Sandy Prentice tried the Ingham pool from the bank. My mother and I were to try the Garden Wall and then the Putt, the bottom pool on the beat. I could hardly wait and was trying a few casts from the bank before the others had finished putting on their waterproof clothing.

I am sorry to say that it was a rather deflated boy who was put ashore at lunch time. I had caught nothing when I had been fishing, but I was sharing a rod with my mother who had landed seven kelts. My father and Mr Prentice had caught three fresh fish between them weighing between six and eight pounds and quite a few kelts. After lunch, Veevers persuaded my father to take me back to the Putt with him while he took my mother and Sandy Prentice back to the upper pools.

Once again we started from the Garden Wall but neither of us moved a fish there. Then we dropped downstream in the boat to try the Putt. Not long after starting my father got a pull, and shortly afterwards he hooked an eight pound fish which was soon landed. He was very disappointed that I had not caught it, but Oliver thought that the best chance for me was lower down in the pool where the kelts had been taking in the morning, so he persuaded my father to fish for a bit longer before handing over the rod.

Ten minutes later another fish took, a much heavier one this time, which weighed twenty-three pounds when it was landed. Oliver was highly delighted because in those days a spring fish of that size was quite exceptional and even more so because it had sea lice on it. After the fish were stowed in the boat, they both insisted that I tried my luck and very soon afterwards I landed my first Tweed salmon. It was only six pounds but the fact that I had killed a fish was really all that mattered to me. I was tired and cold and anything, even a kelt, would have been acceptable to me at that time.

I fished on for quite a while afterwards but nothing else moved to my sprat and eventually I handed the rod back to my father who suddenly caught two fish, rip, rap, almost on his last fishable casts in the pool not far above the weir.

We finished the afternoon with five clean fish and no sign of a kelt, in strange contrast to the morning's fishing of the same water when we had seven kelts and no fresh fish.

When we joined the rest of our party we found that Mr Prentice had had no success, but my mother had been lucky enough to kill two clean fish. So, as it turned out, seven fresh fish were killed in the afternoon and no kelts, whereas in the morning we had had three fresh fish and about a dozen kelts between us. We had had an excellent days sport by any standards. Both boatmen thought more of the twenty-three pound fish than all the others put together. That night in the hotel all the fishing party were celebrating a very productive day's sport, as most of them had got into double figures. However, before bedtime, hopes of a similar day on Saturday faded as the rain started to come down again. In the morning, sure enough, the river was rising and it became increasingly discoloured as the day progressed. We fished hard all day and had numerous pulls, something that often happens on a rising river but we only landed two kelts and one fresh fish which was caught by Mr Prentice.

By mid-afternoon the river was once again a raging torrent, no doubt a good omen for Mr Prentice who was staying on for another

76

The Bridge pool (Junction beat) – River Tweed.

week, but slightly frustrating for us. After all, we had only had one day's fishing when conditions were suitable out of the six, but that day had more than made up for the rest. It could well have been far worse and in angling one has to learn to accept what comes. As the other man says 'you pay your money and accept the conditions that the Lord provides'.

My story of the Tweed was prompted by my early memories of Sandy Prentice. He taught me from a very early age to persist and always be optimistic when fishing. He was undoubtedly the most persistent angler I ever knew, and was remarkably successful on days of most atrocious conditions. He was one of these extra-ordinary people who seemed to get a new lease of life when he saw other anglers going home, and it seemed to give him an incentive to fish even harder. He rarely packed up until darkness forced him, even during the period of his life when I knew him, as he was over sixty-five when I was born and nearly eighty when we fished the Tweed.

Of all the qualities needed by an angler if he is to be successful the most important are patience, persistence and first and fore-most, optimism.

In all salmon fishing there is only really one hopeless condition or time of day when an angler has absolutely no chance of catching a fish, and that is when his fly or lure is not in the water. Quite regardless of water or weather conditions there is always a chance of catching a salmon as long as you are fishing.

There is absolutely no doubt that the angler who persists and keeps his fly or lure in the water for the longest time will in the end be best rewarded. Anglers who try to anticipate when salmon are likely to take on a certain day, or at a certain time, are taking a risk and inevitably by doing so they reduce their chances. Although, under ideal conditions, they will quite often hit it right and kill fish, they have little or no chance of success if the fish either do the unexpected or else conditions suddenly change for the better.

A persistent and patient angler is always present when a run of fish suddenly enters his beat; he is in position to observe all that is going on and has complete continuity of knowledge throughout his fishing period, where the fish are and what they are doing. For this reason he can usually fish in the right place at the right time even if he has not got the benefit of intimate knowledge of the stretch of water he is fishing. Continual observation teaches all fishermen a great deal. On the other hand, the angler who fishes only intermittently during his fishing holiday has little idea of what has happened before, and unless he knows his water really well he will have to rely on luck if he is to be in the right place at the right time.

The optimist always hopes the unexpected will happen. He believes even under the most useless conditions that he will find the 'fool of the family' and therefore he is most likely to persist in conditions when the majority pack in and go home. It is extraordinary how often this type of angler is rewarded for his patience no matter how much the dice seem'to be loaded against him. The optimist is also extremely likely to find fish and catch them in unusual places. Optimists will fish every nook and cranny of their beat hoping against hope that a fish will be in one of them and in the end they will very often strike lucky. Over the years the number of fish that they kill in either utterly hopeless conditions or unusual places mount up to an appreciable quantity, and so their optimism and keenness never dies away.

I must admit that I am myself an incurable optimist and, especially when I had more time in my younger days, spent every moment of the day on the river regardless of whether I was catching anything or not. I was always trying something unusual or experimenting in some shape or form and believe that what may have seemed long wasted periods of time in those days has held me in excellent stead throughout my long fishing career.

I well remember coming home on holiday from school to the Welsh Dee one year at the end of March, only to find that my father's water had been given to the Duke of Westminster's party for a few days. This did not accord with my plans, and so I pestered my father to ask a friend of his who lived at the head of the valley just below Lake Bala and owned a small beat of the Dee, to see whether I could go and fish there. This beat was never normally fished until June and as this was the end of March both my father and his friend told me I had no hope of catching anything at all. Nevertheless I was quite happy to go and cast a fly on the water. How wrong they both were. Not only did I kill a fresh run nine pound salmon in the morning, but caught another, a twenty-eight pound fish just before I packed up in the evening. Never before had a fish been caught on that beat before the 20th May. It only goes to show that you can never tell unless you try.

I remember another occasion on the Cassley after a very hard winter. The river was completely frozen on 28th January, but on that evening the weather turned mild with torrential rain overnight. In the morning the river was a huge flood showing seven feet on the gauge with ice floes floating down. However, by mid-day the colour was beginning to clear, and although there was still a lot of ice floating on the surface I decided to venture out and have a cast, undeterred by my keeper's advice to leave it till the morning.

I tried one or two high water pools below the bridge and then came down to the Lower House pool where there was a short stretch of fishable water close to the bank. On my third cast I felt a strong pull and I was into a fish. I thought it was bound to be a kelt and was fairly hard on it until I saw the golden glint as it turned near the surface of the water, I then knew that it was a fresh one. I never had more fun playing a fish in my life, as I had to manoeuvre my line out of the way of big tables of ice as they sped past on the current and tried to keep a tight line on the fish at the same time. When I eventually landed it, we threw it on top of a large wall of ice lying on the bank and took a photograph of it.

I do not think even I would have been foolish enough to venture forth on a day of such hopeless conditions except that in those days there was great rivalry between the rivers flowing into the Kyle of Sutherland. All the ghillies and proprietors tried to outdo the others by catching the first fish of the season. When the word got round that I had caught one on the 29th January, no-one could believe that anyone would have been stupid enough to fish that day with the river in flood, full of ice floes, let alone be lucky enough to catch one as well. So the evidence of my photograph was most welcome.

Fishing can be full of frustrations and water or weather conditions can both make a river practically unfishable at times. When this occurs as a result of drought, particularly in the summer, a river can be out of order for a considerable period. Another quality that anglers must have therefore is a mild temperament to help them endure with patience if they happen to hit these conditions on their fishing trip.

It is very easy to decide to cancel a fishing trip when you hear that conditions are absolutely hopeless. But I don't think you should allow these reports to stop you going. And when you arrive and discover how bad things really are, don't pack up and return home before the end of your holiday. For it is when conditions suddenly change that you can have the day all anglers dream about when large numbers of salmon are caught or even records broken.

In this country many of our rivers do not have very large catchment areas and because of that large amounts of rain are not required before rivers rise appreciably. It is therefore perfectly possible for conditions in many river systems to be transformed almost overnight when the weather changes, and a river that is in hopeless order one day can be in reasonable order the next and in absolutely perfect condition a day or so afterwards.

In the spring and summer particularly when fresh fish are running the rivers, it is almost a certainty in drought conditions that large numbers of fish will accumulate offshore or in the estuaries waiting for the right water conditions so that they can ascend the rivers of their origin. When the first spate arrives these fish come rushing into the river and when water conditions settle and are favourable for fishing, the fish are available to be caught. It is when this occurs that you can have the day of your lifetime and if you have not had the patience to wait and hope that a change in the weather will come, you might hear that record bags were made the day after you have returned home.

That Friday on the Tweed was a case in point. It would have been easy for us all to pack up and go home on the Tuesday or Wednesday of that week. The conditions of mud and coloured river were really almost hopeless and if we had not had the frost on Thursday night then I am sure we would have had a blank week. And we might well have been justified in a decision to pack up and go home. In the event the persistence shown by Sandy Prentice and my father paid off and I would recommend this spirit of perseverance to all fishermen.

April on the Cassley, 1957 and a March day on the Oykel

The winter of 1956–7 had been reasonably mild with a few short periods of sharp frost, and there had been little or no snow even on the higher mountains. Late February had been a bit wetter with mild south-westerly winds, and this mild weather had melted what snow there was. During this time a few fish had run into the rivers of the north and we had caught several on the Rosehall beat.

Early in March a high pressure area formed over Scandinavia which dominated the weather over northern Scotland. Bright sunny days followed in succession with hard frosts every night and a strong east wind. The water level in the rivers fell rapidly and by the middle of the month the Cassley was so low that fish were unable to enter the mouth of the river and had to lie off in the Kyle waiting for the water levels to rise.

The east wind and dry weather continued throughout March save on the 27th, when a drizzle from the east raised the water level by six inches. A few fish thenpushed into the river and during the last three days of March and the first days of April, we killed fifteen fish. On Saturday, 7th April, I had asked a friend who was staying with his family over at Dornoch to come and fish, and he was also due to fish with his father on Monday the 9th. On Thursday, April 5th I rang him to say that conditions were hopeless, but he determined to come.

Saturday duly arrived. It was a most unpromising looking day. The river was dead low and there was a strong north-east wind. In fact we were lucky. Gideon Rutherford my friend, caught a nice fish backing up the Upper Platform pool from the far side in the morning, and late in the evening he came with a twenty pound salmon, a very big fish for the Cassley, caught in the Gravel pool, where my father had moved a big fish the day before.

That Saturday night when I went to bed was dry and cold, but on waking the next morning I heard the rain beating against the west-facing window of my bedroom. The weather had changed at last and prospects for the coming week could only be good. All salmon fishermen will know how we felt kept from the river that Sunday. The fish pent for so long in the Kyle could be seen moving up the river in quantities, and by the evening the river had settled to the perfect fishing height of two feet and the rain had eased off.

Next morning the gauge read two feet three inches but to my dismay it was raining again and judging by the pools on the drive must have been raining for some time overnight. We were therefore faced with what was likely to be a rising river, something I have always dreaded at the best of times, and when this was the first good water we had had for over a month it was frustrating to say the least.

Six of us split into pairs. Willie Mackay the keeper would go with my father and fish the bottom beat. I would take Major Rutherford to the top beat on the left bank, while Menzies would take Gideon and fish the right bank having first fished the Bridge pool on the way up.

I started with the Major at the Upper Platform pool and half-way down the pool he hooked a fish, which after sundry adventures we eventually netted out. I could see that the river was now rising rapidly, but in spite of this we caught another fish each in the Upper Platform pool and then we moved up river to the Round pool and the Run. The rest of the morning was like a fairy tale dream with fish coming to the fly virtually every cast. Major Rutherford and I caught a further eight fish making eleven in all, two in the Run, four from the Round pool and the first two of the season from the Cemetary pool and we must have lost or pulled as many again.

Gideon and Menzies never got above the Upper Platform pool they were moving so many fish there. They caught six fish from it, including one of twenty-eight pounds and they had had another fish from the Bridge pool first thing in the morning. My father and Willie had landed six fish on the bottom beat making a total catch of twenty-four fish in the morning, and all this while the river had risen a further sixteen inches.

Lunch, as you might imagine, was a hurried meal and we returned to find the river running at four feet six inches. This meant that many of the best pools were now too high and only the tails of the quieter longer pools were fishable, and one or two odd corners close into the banks. The heavens were open and the rain teemed down all the while but in spite of this we caught a further ten fish, mostly from the Run where my father and Willie caught five, with another three being taken from the opposite bank. This made the total for the day thirty-four fish, easily a record for the beat at that time, and I would say that we pulled or lost an equal number of fish. Obviously this only happened because of the many fish which entered the river having been cooped in the Kyle for so long, and also a large number of fresh fish had been drawn in to the river straight from the sea by the first high water.

That evening we all thought that it was a once in lifetime's happening but we were to be surprised again. The following day, again two friends were coming to fish with us and although the river was down to three feet three inches in the morning, it was raining again. The river rose by two feet during the day but in spite of this we killed thirty-five fish beating the previous day's record by one. And this is the more surprising when you consider that two of the fishermen, my father and Menzies were seventy-seven and eighty years old respectively, and therefore not able to fish particularly hard.

Wednesday of that week the river at last began to settle and these conditions lasted for the rest of the time. That day we killed twenty-seven fish and then fourteen, nine and five respectively. The first two days when the river was rising we killed sixty-nine fish, and rose or lost almost as many. The last four days when fifty-five fish were killed, only four were lost or pulled. This is a supremely good example of how a rising river upsets the taking pattern of salmon and there is no doubt that if we had had settled water on either of the first two days we might well have had over fifty fish in a day.

I have never before or since seen fish take the way they did on those two days on any sort of rising river. I am sure the reason why they did was because the whole of the spring run of the river, which normally would enter the river system over the six week period from March to the middle of April, came in two days. As the first day that they were able to run the river was a Sunday the fish had a chance to settle in the pools before anyone else fished for them. There were very few fish in the river and so the fresh fish had the chance of occupying the best taking lies when they were new from the sea.

Many fishermen that I know do not realise how important this factor can be in salmon fishing, and it is particularly important in the smaller rivers where the pools and taking places are small and

Bridge Pool – River Cassley.
A famed high water pool.

relatively few. The first fish into a pool will take up the best lies and the later arrivals have to make do with less preferred positions. Eventually these fish will be pricked, be hooked and lost, or just become wary of the fisherman's lures. They are then 'stale' and uncatchable. In any pool there will only be a number of lies that will produce fish because the fly or lure will only work properly or attractively in a proportion of any piece of water. Once a fish has become stale in its lie it will guard it against any intruder and often, quite literally, be afraid to jump or move in it for fear of being usurped. Only when a big flood forces the fish to move in the pool or when fresh water makes them move upstream will a reshuffle take place, and the best taking places in a pool again become profitable from the angler's point of view.

This theory is confirmed by the following facts which are typical of what can happen on the Rosehall beat of the Cassley when the water temperatures remain below 45°F into April. One of the best taking pools is the Round pool at the head of which is a steep, small fall which the fish will not surmount until the water temperature rises above 45°F. Often the first fish of the season is taken from this pool. One season from the 11th January until the 27th March we killed sixty-nine fish, twenty-seven of which were from the Round pool. That year from the 27th March until the 23rd April not a single fish was killed in the Round pool, although we caught one hundred and six more fish in the pools below, thirty-three from the Run which lies only fifteen or so yards downstream. Also during all this time we never saw a fish move in the pool although sea-liced fish were taken in the pool below, and we saw fish running through the Run and into the Round pool. On the 24th April fish appeared in the Cemetery pool, the pool above the Round pool, for the first time and that day we killed eleven fish in the Round pool itself and a further twenty-nine fish in the next six fishing days, while on the whole beat we killed eighty-nine salmon – the stale fish had at last vacated their lies.

In general one of the reasons why spring fishing can be so good, assuming that there is any sort of spring run, is that there has been no large build up of stale fish. The best taking lies are usually occupied by fresh fish who are constantly forcing their way up river and therefore are readily attracted to the angler's lures. They do not have time to get stale in a pool.

Very often on the opening day of the season on rivers such as the Aberdeenshire Dee, where fish come in all through the period from October – 31st January, a large number of fish are caught, as the angler will be covering fish which are seeing a fly or spinner for the first time. They have not had time to become educated. After a while these fish are not so easily caught and the angler has to rely on the fresh run springers to keep their catches up.

In a way the week I have written about was very like the opening of the salmon season on a river compressed and fore-shortened. There were on the 7th April that year very, very few fish in the river and therefore a large number of the best taking lies were unoccupied. The flood that brought them in on Sunday also would have shifted those fish that were in the river out of the best lies, and so the multitude of fresh fish arriving had an equal chance of occupying the best taking lies in the river. As the week went on, although we had good water, and at the end of the week near perfect fishing conditions, the catches dropped and the fish that were caught came from small pots and corners as, by then, the main taking lies were occupied by 'stale fish'. The statistics for this week are as follows. Out of the thirty-four fish caught on the Monday, twenty-nine came from the main taking pools on the beat with seven of them being caught in the Round pool where we must have lost almost as many there. After that day we only killed a further two fish in the Round pool and we only killed twelve out of thirty-five in the main holding pools on Tuesday, fourteen out of twenty-seven on Wednesday, and three out of twenty-eight in the last three days of the week. Perhaps I should add for the benefit of those readers who do not know the Cassley, that there was no question of any fish running through the beat as the water temp-erature was below 48°F. No fish were therefore running up the Falls above the Cemetery pool as they cannot be ascended until 48°F is reached, and the Falls above that cannot be ascended until the temperature reaches 52°F. Another point worth mentioning as a further proof is that on the first three days of the week a large number of the fish we caught were 'stale', and by this I mean without sea lice, and were those fish that had been held back in the Kyle by the low water, while on the last three days every fish we caught had long-tailed sea lice and were straight out of the sea.

I always remember when as a young and inexperienced angler fishing one of the best beats of one of the most famous Scottish rivers with a very experienced old ghillie. We first of all fished down one of the main holding pools which was full of fish. It was in perfect order and I never moved a fish in all the forty-five minutes that it took me to cover the pool. As I climbed out of the water at the tail I took out my fly box and asked my companion which fly I should put on for a second try down the pool. Much to my surprise he told me that it was not worth a change of fly, and not worth fishing down again, 'It is not a change of fly you are wanting, it is a change of fish, and all these buggers have been pricked in the mouth lower down.'

He then marched me off to an insignificant-looking little pool which he explained was merely a resting pool but there might, just might, be a fresh fish in it resting on its way up river. Well, we were lucky and there was a fresh run grilse of six pounds in the pool, covered with sea lice, and we caught another fresh fish in a similar pool later in the day. But not a touch did we have in all the famous pools on the beat, hard though I fished, tantalised and tormented by the feverish activity in all of them.

The lesson to be learnt from all this is never, never waste too much time on the big holding pools on your beat, however many fish you see in them. This is particularly true in the autumn when there are, inevitably, a lot of stale fish about. Fish the big pools certainly, and even back them up, but if you are not successful quickly move on to the next pool and pay particular attention to the small runs and pots where the odd fish may be found resting as very often these fish are far easier to catch than those in the main holding pools on the beat. If you have time, it can make sense in high water when fish may be moving upstream during the day, to fish these pots quickly more than once during that time as you never know when a fish might have just entered the pool. And in low water it can be worth giving them a flick late in the evening as fish very often push up river for a pool or two as dusk falls.

On the other hand, never, never leave a pool where you are catching fish, unless you intend to return to that pool in the very near future. Keep your eyes open and try to see what the fish are doing on a particular day. If you see fish that are obviously running through a pool try and find out where they are resting that day. In the spring particularly it is quite common to find a run of fish all resting in the same pool on one day.

I had an interesting example of this four years ago on the Oykel. I was fishing the Langwell beat early in March with three friends from Lincolshire. The river was a good height at two feet six inches and in excellent order. In the morning two of my friends went with the ghillie to the bottom of the beat to fish the Whirl, Brae pool and

A typical rock pool.

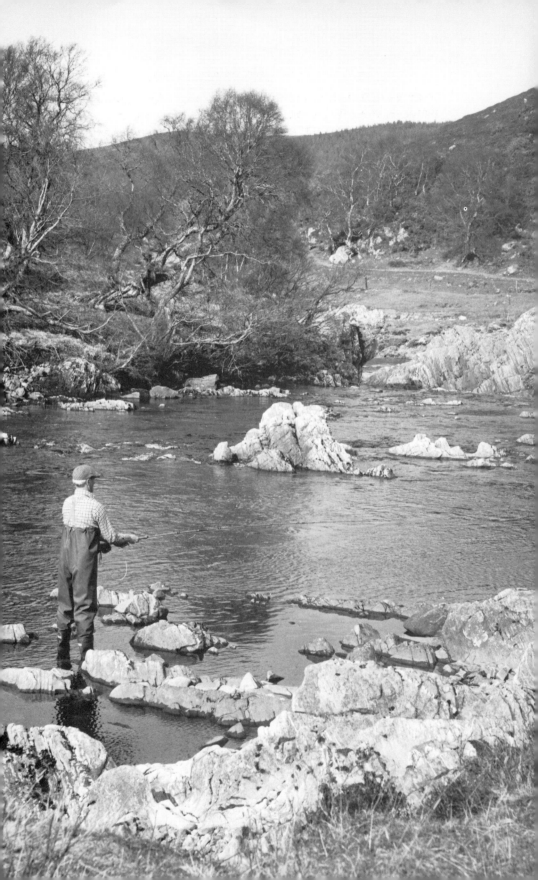

Brae burn while I stayed at the top of the beat fishing Langwell and the Dyke pools.

We did not move a fish in Langwell although I saw several fish cut the water above and just below the suspension bridge, obviously running fish. I therefore suggested that we go down and try the Dyke pool which we did. Again we had no response and when we all met at Langwell for lunch it was the same story from the bottom party. I was puzzled by this. We could see fish moving in Langwell which were definitely running fish and it did not seem to me to be likely that the fish were not resting somewhere in the beat. The water was high and Langwell is too long a beat for salmon to push right on through it in one day that early in the spring.

I had thought that the fish were probably resting in the tail of the Brae, or Whirl pool, but my companions had seen nothing in either of these places. After lunch we swopped over and I went down to the bottom pools. We fished all of these thoroughly but apart from one fish which we saw move at the tail of the Brae pool we saw and felt nothing.

By now it was getting late and my companion said that he was tired and would go home. I then went back to the top of the river to see how the others were faring but the answer was not a move, although they had seen fish showing in Langwell. I was irritated by this and resolved to try once more down below before darkness fell. Taking Johnnie Macleod with me as ghillie I went back to the Dyke pool and as we got there I suggested to him that possibly the fish were resting in the Upper Dyke pool. This pool was generally hardly worth fishing, as it usually only killed one or two fish in a season. It was normally a deep slow pool but with the river at that height there was a good current flowing through it that day. Johnnie's response was not really printable but the gist of it was that he doubted it, and even if they were the pool was virtually unfishable from the left-hand bank as it was lined by alders which made casting impossible. The pool was normally fished from the right-hand bank, the farm side, and we did not have time to get round as dusk was approaching.

I started therefore backing up the tail of the Lower Dyke pool and finally, after about fifteen casts, I hooked a fish which we landed. The blank was, at last, saved. I backed up the Lower Dyke again and then ignoring Johnnie's protests pushed my way through the alders along the bank of the Upper Dyke pool. Well you all know what to expect, and suffice it to say that I landed another four fish from that pool before darkness fell that night. It isn't a story that I am proud of, for if only I had made certain that the whole beat had been fished that day, at the outset, everyone might have had a fish, but it illustrates how very important it is to cover all of the beat, even those pools which are normally worthless.

The Inver and Two Conundrums

If you drive to the west coast of Scotland, past Loch Assynt towards Lochinver you will pass down the banks of the Inver. It is a short river like so many that flow into the sea off the west coast of Scotland, but it is one of the most fascinating that I have been lucky enough to fish in my long fishing career. The reason for this is the variety of pools. There are, as you would imagine, a number of small rocky pools but there are also larger pools that would not disgrace a far more substantial water with streamy heads and gliding tails. In addition there are a succession of man-made pools with large concrete and stone weirs that stretch across the width of the river. Lastly, there is a small loch near the head of the river called Loch an Iasgaich, which is probably the most productive pool on the whole river which can be fished both from a boat and from the bank.

The Inver flows out of Loch Assynt, a long loch famous for the betrayal of Montrose and for its large trout. As most of the head-waters run from the bare mountains of the region Brabeck, Ben Huron and Glencanisp, desolate and barren, the water is usually gin clear, save for the first spate after a long drought in the summer. Fishing begins in earnest in June as there is no real spring run, but from then on fish enter the river and sport can be very good.

The first time that I fished the Inver was one July early in the 1950s. I drove over taking Willie Mackay, the Rosehall keeper with me, and as we motored west we saw that the burns were more and more swollen denoting heavy overnight rain. This was not really surprising, although it had been dry overnight at Rosehall, as the weather in the west coast of the north of Scotland is unpredictable to say the least but it was a good sign. Sure enough our optimistic thoughts were echoed by Murdo Ross our ghillie, who was at that time the head keeper on the Assynt estate. Murdo was a real character with the enchanting nickname of 'my Bonnie Boy'. Not only did he have a wide knowledge of fishing, shooting and stalking but he also knew all of the local history of Assnyt, and he could translate all the Gaelic names of the burns, corries, and mountains and explain why they had been named as such in the first place.

Murdo said that there had been heavy rain the previous afternoon but that the river was now settled and beginning to drop so that conditions should be just right. We started fishing at the Ladder pool which had the reputation of being one of the best on the river. This pool is most attractive to fish as it is at the head of a long narrow gorge. It is a narrow pool and you stand above the water so that you can see you fly working as it crosses the current. That day only the tail was really fishable as the river was too high, but as I worked my way down the pool two fish came at my flies at once, without touching me, and the next cast a much bigger fish also moved to my flies without taking. I fished on down and then started to back the pool up. As I reached the place where I had moved the bigger fish, it came up and took solidly and after an exciting quarter of an hour I drew him safely into Murdo's net. This fish was only two or three days out of the sea and weighed sixteen pounds.

After that we all fished the pool again in turns and between us we moved another seven fish, all of whom came to the fly but none of them opened their mouth to take it. We could see the fish come to within an inch or so of the fly and then turn away, and this activity was clearly visible to us in the clear water.

This was puzzling. There was no ostensible reason why the fish should behave like this. The river was now dropping and there was no thunder in the air. On the contrary it was a good fishing day with a cool, but not strong, south-west wind, and there were fresh fish in the river, for we could clearly distinguish the sea lice on a number of fish from our vantage point above the Ladder pool. Also the day was not too sunny but on the contrary had good cloud cover with bright periods when the sun was out, and the river was a perfect height for the beat.

There was therefore no apparent cause for the fish to be unsettled. But unsettled they were, for the same pattern of behaviour was obvious in all the pools that we fished up till lunch. In every pool we moved fish, by lunchtime we counted nineteen that had come to our flies, but, apart from the sixteen pounder from the Ladder pool, not a single fish had touched a fly. And the afternoon was exactly the same, except that we moved fewer fish, only seven, without a single touch.

To complete the puzzle I was fishing with a floating line with a No. 9 double-hooked Sweep on the dropper and a No. 6 Hairy Mary in the tail position to start with, although I changed my flies during the day, while Willie and Murdo who were sharing a rod were using a No. 5 sunk Kingfisher line. They started with a No. 8 shrimp fly and also changed their flies from the sublime to the ridiculous as the saying goes. We also fished in every style that we could think of, working the fly, fishing fast, fishing slow, backing up and letting the fly come across the pool without any imparted motion. The fish seemed to be quite impartial and we moved something to practically every fly we tried and every method had some response but no fish appeared to want to take the fly solidly.

The second day on the Inver from which I want to draw a fishing moral, if that is the right word, occurred some twenty years later in the 1970s. I was invited to fish the same beat in late June and my ghillie on that day was Charlie Ross, a man I had known nearly all my life as he had been an underkeeper at Rosehall in the 1930s. I was very fond of Charlie who was another of nature's gentlemen.

When we met on the river bank he told me that the river was dead low, a marked contrast to the first day that I have described, but that a few fish were poking into the bottom pools with the tide and he was hopeful that we might meet with some success in the rocky, streamy pools below the Star. I was fishing with a floating line and two flies, my normal No. 9 Hairy Mary on the dropper and a minuscule blue and black tube with a size 16 treble in the tail position. Charlie was in favour of the Hairy Mary but disapproved of my tube fly which he thought was much too small even for that height of water. To start with we had no success. We fished the necks at the top of the New pool, then in succession the Star, Pollan and the Gravestones. When we got to the Ladder pool Charlie wanted to change my fly again but I insisted in persevering and promptly hooked a nice grilse which was soon netted out. At this point Charlie said that we should rest the pool for it would have been too disturbed when I played the fish in the very low water. I will return to this point later, but suffice it to say that in this instance I agreed in deference to Charlie's wishes. We were very lucky that day and I landed a second grilse shortly afterwards from the Hogs Back pool. This was a memorable fish. You fish the Hogs Back from a wooden platform and from which you can see right down into the pool. First cast I saw a fish come at my tail fly, but just as it was about to open its mouth to take the tube another fish rose at the fly right across the nose of the first fish. Both missed the fly but the first fish kept swimming forward and ignoring the tail fly, its original target, took the dropper, something I have never seen happen before or since.

Now let me return to the first day. I know that salmon are the most unpredictable and uncertain of quarries but nevertheless I am convinced that there is usually some explanation for their behaviour if you look hard enough. Most experienced fishermen will have had days when the fish have consistently come short and either just plucked the fly or, more annoyingly, seemingly been well hooked but after a few minutes play, drop off. On many of these days the angler can count himself lucky if he lands one fish to save the blank in spite of numerous offers.

Usually there is a good reason for the fish coming short in this fashion. The most common and I have seen it on many, many occasions is when the river is rising, or bumping up and down with frequent rain showers. Then I am sure the fish do not settle into their lies and when they move to the fly do so without that single minded determination that we all like to see and experience. The other occasion when fish come short is a corollary of the first case, or rather very often a corollary, which is when fish are running. I am not saying that running fish cannot be caught, they can, but very often they just move to the fly or pluck it and on days when this happens it is like a disease which affects the whole river.

Since the 1960s there is another instance which I am sure affects the way in which fish take. That is the outbreak of UDN. I am convinced that when the disease is present in the fish's system they often take short and fluff the fly, even when water conditions are ideal.

However, while it is a fact that fish very often take short on a rising or unsettled river, I am not convinced that it is the cause and effect. Many experienced ghillies and fishermen that I know feel that it is not the water conditions which matter but the changes in acidity or the chemical make-up of the water that accompanies these conditions. When a river rises sharply, particularly after a long period of drought, it becomes markedly more acid with sharply increased mud and peat content in the water. I am sure that this sickens the fish and makes them more lethargic when they move to the fly.

On many of the west coast rivers of Scotland which have considerable runs of sea trout I know a number of ghillies who believe that sea trout which, contrary to salmon, feed in fresh water do not take a fly readily after a spate, but will take it freely one or two days afterwards. This has invariably been my experience, and the third day after a good spate has a magical significance to a number of fishermen I know.

I have heard fishermen swear that the acidity has nothing to do with it and that the reason for any shortcoming on the part of the fish was because of poor visibility in spate-coloured water. Personally I do not believe this, as I know how good is the sight and judgement of all fish and even in the dirtiest spate it is remarkable how clear the river appears if you fill a glass with the opaque and muddy water.

On the first day I conclude that the fish were still suffering from the increased acidity of the water and while I think it strange, indeed very strange, that we moved so many fish with only one taking the fly, I am sure this was the real reason. If all anglers think back to their own experience, and this is often more applicable to lochs and still water than rivers, there are days when you will move, or have moved, a large number of fish and landed very few. There are other days when you hook and land nearly every fish you rise. This is certainly my own experience on the Kyle and probably more common than we all realise. On that day the first pool we fished enabled us to see right down into the water and observe precisely what the fish were doing, and I think it was a fair assumption that the fish in the other pools were behaving in the same way. If we hadn't had that advantage we would not have known definitely that the fish were moving to, but not taking, the fly under water, and this happens more often than we think.

The second conundrum or question to which I now want to return is when I had just killed my first fish in the Ladder pool on the second day. If I had been alone I would have immediately fished the pool again and it was only in deference to Charlie that I did not. He wanted to rest it. Who is right?

Well I am pretty sure that I am. Charlie and his followers would argue that the disturbance of the fish being played, particularly in the very low water that we had, combined with the movement of the angler and his ghillie up and down the bank, would put down any other fish that might have taken at that time. The best chance therefore would be for the angler to rest the pool and give the putative taking fish a chance to come back on the feed.

The other school of thought holds that for a large period of the day salmon lie in a sort of trance when they are virtually impossible to

The famous Perch and Einaig Fall Pool – Lower Oykel.

catch on any sort of lure. Only a fish that is alert and moving is likely to take. It follows from this that if you hook and play a fish in a pool the occupants of the pool will be awakened from their trance and therefore the effect is going to be beneficial rather than detrimental. All the people who taught me to fish believed this and I have found it to be true particularly so in the very low water conditions of high summer. If you hook a fish in a pool then you will very often hook another straight away and sometimes it will be a fish of a similar size, in all probability the mate of the first fish. I would therefore urge all anglers in the summer, if they hook and land a fish to go straight back to the head of the pool and fish it down again, and they will be surprised how often a second fish comes their way.

When I was a boy and lived in Wales there was a friend of my father's, the Major, who used to fish the beat downstream of ours on the Welsh Dee. It was his invariable practice never to fish his water without his ghillie whom he would command to stone the pool before he started fishing. The ghillie used to do this using a pound weight attached to a long cord. He threw the weight as far across the pool as he could and then he drew the weight ashore. This procedure was repeated every five yards until the tail of the pool was reached. When the ghillie had finished the Major started fishing and if he didn't catch any more fish than anyone else he certainly caught no fewer. His theory, or rather reasoning, was that he wanted any fish that were in the pool to be awake before he started fishing. This was his method of accomplishing this.

I was intrigued by this story which I regarded as pretty far-fetched and I persuaded my father to ask the Major to fish. He duly arrived one Saturday. The river was in fairly good order and we started at the top of the Summer-house pool, a long narrow pool where the main current flowed under our bank. The Major tried to insist that we fished the pool before he did but we told him that we wanted to see the result of stoning the pool. Parry, the Major's ghillie, then took out his cord and weight and worked his way down the pool, throwing his weight across the river and then dragging it back all over the lies. When he had finished the Major started fishing and as he reached the best water at the 'diving stone lie' his line tightened and he was fast into a good fish. When he had landed that fish he started again and promptly hooked another at the 'diamond stone lie', twenty yards further down the pool.

I am bound to say that these were his only successes of the day and I cannot claim that this experiment really proved anything one way or the other. I think it very likely that if either my father or I had fished the pool without stoning it we would have caught the two fish that the Major did. Also the remainder of our water was really too wide for the stone to reach the best lies so could not really be said to have had a fair trial. What it certainly proved was that it did not disturb the fish to the extent that they became uncatchable. On two subsequent occasions I saw the Major catch fish on his own water after the pool had been stoned, and on another occasion he caught several fish in a pool which I had just fished unsuccessfully without the benefit of Parry and his cord and weight.

At other times I have twice in the summer caught fish in a pool within half an hour of the family bathers leaving the water. On another occasion I hooked a salmon literally seconds after an otter had swum down the pool I was fishing, and I know of at least two other people who have had the same experience as this.

I am not going to try to draw any far-reaching or profound conclusion from all this. I will maintain that there is some truth in the idea of waking salmon up, particularly in the summer when water temperatures are high. Personally I would define the word disturb, when applied to salmon in three phases, to alert, to frighten, and lastly to panic. Provided the fish are merely alerted then certainly no harm and possibly some good may be done.

Two Days on the Shin

I have known the Shin nearly all my life and fished it at all times of the year but the two days I am going to describe were in May in early 1960. I had been asked to fish for Colonel MacFarlane who had had to leave two days before his tenancy ended, and as luck would have it the day before I was due to fish there was a full moon.

I am a great believer in new or full moon tides which I believe bring fresh fish in to our northern rivers, and if I am taking people fishing, I always try and do so in a week when one of these tides occurs. So I set off full of hope. My ghillie was Willie Macdonald from Linside, a man who had ghillied on the Lower Shin all his life and knew the river like the back of his hand. We started fishing at the Big Falls pool, with Willie fishing behind me and we worked our way diligently right down river to Big Clarig with no move or sign of a fish. Willie went back upstream to fetch the car while I continued on down river, and we fished every pool down to the Home pool without any success at all.

This was very deflating. After a very late lunch Willie decided that we ahould go down to the Farm pools at the bottom of the river and fish them. This we did. First of all we fished them from the left bank, with two flies each; and then we crossed over and fished them from the right bank below the electrodes at the tail race. We were just about to call it a day when I saw a fish head and tail half way across the pool. I had just changed my fly yet again for a Waddington Hairy Mary with a red flash at its tail and Willie reluctantly agreed that I could give this fly a swim as it was by now nearly six thirty p.m. I had hardly started when I got a pull and soon landed a small fish of six pounds which had been in the river some time. I then started again and I promptly caught a second fish, and then a third. Both these were bigger fish than the first at eighteen and thirteen and a half pounds, but both of them were pretty stale. Had they been in the pool all the time or as I rather suspect had they just come in from the Kyle?

The following day we started again at the tail of the Falls, the only fishable part of the pool. I always try and fish this pool with a very short line as the water is *very rough* with *many buffeting currents* and I think that a short line helps me to keep a better control of my fly. This day nothing came in the Falls pool but below it first Willie, and then I, moved a fish in Culag and then I moved another three fish, one in the Shoulder of Cromarty and two above the big rock at the tail of the Rocky Cast. Not one of these fish touched the fly. We then went down to Big Clarig and right in the tail I hooked a fish which got off after a moment's play.

We then sat down and debated what to do. First of all I changed my fly from a 2/0 Garry Dog to a Hairy Mary of the same size for it seemed to me that while the fish were coming readily enough to the Garry Dog they were fluffing it, and I reasoned that they might take the duller-hued Hairy Mary better. Then I suggested to Willie that we retrace our steps and try all the fish we had moved on the way down again. Willie in the end agreed. We started at the Rocky Cast and every time I covered the place where a fish had moved to the fly, it came up and swallowed it firmly. At lunch we were in the happy position of having five fish on the bank, each one fresh and covered with sea lice. The full moon had certainly done its stuff.

Of course I cannot really really explain why the fish which fluffed the fly on the way down took it so readily only an hour or so later. It could well just have been the change of fly, I admit. But I think that those fish which we caught had so recently arrived in the pools in the morning, that first time down they had not settled in their lies, and this caused them to fluff the fly when they came to it. Certainly if you do move a lot of fish without touching any of them the first fishing of the day, it is always worth retracing your steps and giving these fish a choice of a different fly later in the day. Very often you will succeed if you do this, and if you are pressed for time and want to cover all of your beat thoroughly you need only just fish the lie, six or seven casts to cover the place where the fish move, which can take very little time at all.

That afternoon we returned again to the Farm pools. We started fishing from the left bank without success and then we tried the right bank with no result. But fish were by now moving all over the pools and I was determined to catch one more as I had caught five fish in a day several times on the Shin but never six, and I wanted to beat my record. So I forced Willie to return to the left bank and I could see by the look on his face that he thought it indeed a forlorn hope. I tied on the Waddington which had proved so successful the day before and started high up in the pool opposite the electrodes. After about ten casts I hooked a good fish which weighed twenty-three pounds when it was landed, and a little lower down the pool I hooked and landed another, making seven fish in the day. Both these last two fish were stale and the big one had certainly been in fresh water since February.

I think that this raises two main questions and while I am quite certain I know the answer to one of them I am not so certain about the other. First of all, why was I successful from the right bank of the Farm pool on the first day and the left bank on the second? In my opinion, and I fully admit that this is something that I cannot prove one way or the other, I think it was something to do with the different light conditions on the two days. I think that the angle and intensity of the light can make a substantial difference to the way a river fishes, and on rivers like the Shin which have steep gorges with high banks, one day one bank can be favoured and one day the other. Some pools fish best in the morning and others in the afternoon and it is a rare occurrence to catch a fish in the morning in an afternoon pool and vice-versa.

Dark days with a dull light are definitely detrimental to the pools in the gorge on the Shin and the same applies to some of the pools on the Lower Cassley and other rivers that have this type of conformation. These pools also seldom fish well in the evening when the light is fading. It pays therefore to fish first one bank of your beat, and then if you are unsuccessful and have the access and the time, to try the opposite bank. You never know but this might make all the difference.

The other main point of interest that arose out of my two days on the Shin was that all the fresh fish were caught at the top of the beat and all the stale fish at the bottom. I am sure that I know the answer to this apparent contradiction, and in practice it was a temporary change in the way that salmon ascended the Shin following the completion of the hydro-electric scheme on the river.

The two days that I have recounted were the first two days that I fished the river after the hydro scheme had been completed. This scheme has completely changed the way in which fish ascend the Shin and changed for ever the taking pattern of the pools and the productivity of the beats. At the top of the Shin lies Loch Shin, which is one of the longest and largest lochs in Scotland. Every year Loch Shin would fill during the winter, and melting snow from the high mountains which surround its catchment area would keep it topped up until well on into the summer months. It acted as a huge reservoir, and the river as a result usually ran high until the end of May or the beginning of June, depending on the year. Below the Shin Falls the river really runs through three gorges. For much of the time in pre-hydro days the fish found the water in these gorges too heavy and turbulent for comfort. Therefore apart from those periods when the water flow was low enough for them to inhabit the quieter tails of the Falls, Culag, Shoulder of Cromarty and Angus, they used to lie throughout the bottom beat in Fir Dam, Upper Clarig, Paradise and Piper below the upper gorge; the tail of Little Falls, Blackstone and Lower Clarig below the second gorge; and Smiths, the Bridge and Home pools below what can really be termed the third gorge. And of course they lay in several of the long pools from Hectors downstream to the mouth. In any normal year during the spring period before the river temperature rose above 52°F and the fish would start going over the Shin Falls the fishing on the bottom beat was spread out over a large number of pools. Several of these pools were one to two hundred yards in length and there was a tremendous amount of fishing with a great number of taking lies. For these reasons the Shin, in those days, was regarded as one of the freest taking early rivers in Scotland with a very high catch potential. It was also renowned as a river which held very heavy early fish.

After the hydro scheme all this changed and the two days I described were the first two days where this change became apparent. To start with it was like fishing a strange river, and I really had little idea where the fish were likely to be lying. And I must say that Willie with all his experience of the beat was not all that much wiser than I was.

There were very, very few fish then in the pools which normally would have held fish at that time of year, but the bottom pools, the Farm pools, were full of fish. I know now that this was a purely temporary phenomenon which only occurred in the next two years. The first years after the hydro scheme had been completed the fish seemed confused when they entered the river and hung around in the bottom of the two pools making repeated attempts to enter the tail race where the hydro turbines discharged into the river, but they were prevented by the electrode screens across the mouth. It seemed that the larger fish in particular did this and were unwilling to push on upstream when faced with the abnormally low water. Only the smaller fish appeared willing to push on upstream and here, instead of stopping in the pools below the gorges I have described, they pushed on upstream to one of the pools below the main gorge. In the early months of the year they now push on quietly until they enter the main Falls pool itself where they remain until the water temperature rises above 52°F and they go over the falls. Once they reach the Falls pool I would say that apart from one or two lies at the tail of the Falls pool and right on the lip where it runs out, any fish which rests in the main body of the pool is uncatchable until conditions allow them to continue over the falls and upstream.

A large body of the spring run therefore quite literally goes in to a sanctuary and this has had a great effect on the total of fish that come off that beat in the spring. On the second day the five fish, all covered with sea lice, which I caught in the morning came from pools within one hundred and fifty yards of the main Falls pool. Before the hydro scheme I very much doubt whether this would have been the case and this has been amply borne out by the pattern of catches in the years since.

Another thing that is peculiar to the Shin is that the fish have to be offered a much larger fly than one would expect. Often since the advent of the Collie Dog I have known a four inch Collie used with great effect throughout the season and I would always start fishing there with a much bigger fly than I would use elsewhere. This is particularly true of the pools in the gorge and I am sure the reason is because so many of the fish there are running through, and are not truly settled in the pools. If fish are running it can often pay to fish with a ridiculously large fly, for I think that a running fish is more likely to be distracted by something of a good size. This situation appears to hold throughout the year on the Shin.

The final major tragedy brought about by the hydro scheme on the Shin is the changing pattern of the run and spawning grounds, before the hydro the early runs pushed on through the Upper beat and into Loch Shin. Later in the year these fish entered the burns flowing between and into Lochs Merkland, Ghriama and Shin for spawning and only a small proportion of the total stock of fish in the river spawned in the Shin itself. Although the hydro scheme included two Borland fish passes, one on the main dam and one on the diversionary dam at Lairg, neither of these worked very successfully and few, if any, fish now ascend these dams in any one year.

The result is that the main spawning areas of the river are now unused, and the total stock of fish has to spawn in the redds that lie between the diversion dam and the Falls pool. The main spawning places are the redds near the Ladies and Wood pools. In practice there are far too many fish for this limited spawning area and this is a fact which is recognised by the Fishery Board who net out and strip a large number of the fish each autumn.

The Fishery Board then stock the upper waters of the Loch and the headwaters of the Grudie burn with eyed ova or fry and this stocking now supplements the number of fish that return to the river as a result of natural spawning. The practical result of this is a marked decline in the spring run of the Shin while correspondingly the run of summer fish and grilse has increased. This pattern can be found on nearly every river which has been affected by a hydro scheme.

On balance, as I reflect on all this, I am not sure that I am right to condemn the hydro scheme completely. On the Shin I would even say that the total catch on the whole river has increased, for whereas formerly many fish would pass through the Upper beat and into the loch, now penned in the pools below the dam the catch of the upper beat is much greater. Similarly, while the catch from the lower beat is markedly less in the spring, the overall catch is probably around the same for more summer fish and grilse are caught than ever before. And as on so many hydro rivers the constant water flows, even if they are of a fairly low level, do provide water to fish in throughout the summer. While on other rivers, in summers like 1983, the rivers would really be unfishably low for a good number of weeks.

What I do regret on the Shin, quite apart from the loss of the majority of the spring run, is the lack of any real spate conditions, and therefore the loss to the fisherman of so much of what was good fishing water. I do think that in this case the hydro board could lower the level of the compensation flow and then release more water to coincide with periods of natural rainfall so that once in a while a real flood condition would be simulated. This would make the fish change their lies and also bring into play again those lovely pools which are now dead and useless to the fisherman.

I don't see why this shouldn't be done. If, and when it is, I will beg, borrow or buy a day for the pleasure of fishing those pools once again. Today I find fishing the Shin tedious and monotonous in a way, for I know what the height of the water will be and I know there will be few surprises or changes in store for me.

The Conon

For many years a fishing friend of mine, Bob Badden, used to invite me to fish the Coul beat of the River Conon for a day during the first fortnight of July, at the height of the grilse run. I always looked forward to this day because Bob always asked Ian Aird, who is a another great friend, and my late keeper Willie MacKay to fish as well. This day was one we all enjoyed, one of those days when the catch mattered least of all. This was always the final day of the year on which all four of us fished together and it was the climax of many days' companionship by the river.

Bob was postmaster at the little village of Marybank just beside Moy Bridge which carries the main west coast road over the Conon. He knew the whole of the Conon intimately and after it was harnessed by the Hydro-Electric Board for the generation of electricity, he used to contact the generating engineer at Torachilty Power Station to find out the generating schedule on the days when he was going to fish. This was important because if no generation took place the river would run at normal compensation flow, which in the summer was an adequate fishing height, but if either of the turbines were switched on the water level would rise considerably. If you knew that this was going to happen, or due to happen, during the course of the day it enabled you to plan your day at the river bank better. The Coul beat lies on the left bank opposite the Upper Fairburn beat and runs from the Torachilty dam downstream to the junction of the River Blackwater and the Conon. At the top of the beat, under the dam, the current flows to the right bank of the river and on this section of the beat the pools are wide and wooded on the left bank. Here the Fairburn side has the advantage. However, from the tail of the Gillanders pool, the Deer Fence pool and the streams below it and the New pool, the advantage shifts to the Coul side as the current follows the left bank. Below these pools there is a very attractive large, wide pool

with a broad streamy head called the Clachoil. In those days
Fairburn had a boat on it but Coul did not, and for that reason
Coul could only fish the first eighty yards of the pool as hazel trees
lined the left bank. There were two clearances which had been cut
to allow access from the Coul side lower down in the pool, and
some distance further downstream there were two or three small
pools at the bottom of the beat which were only fished if the main
part of the beat proved unproductive.

Most of the fishable water on the Coul side consists of narrow
deep gullies running through a wide rock ledge, ideal water for
holding fish in the summertime and usually very productive during
the grilse run. However, both the New pool and Clachoil are deep
holding pools which fish at any height of water. The wide streamy
heads of both these pools are particularly good in low water and
the tails fish best when the river is high.

Coul is a two rod beat and Bob and I used to fish one rod, with
Ian and Willie sharing the other. One party fished from Gillanders
down to the New pool in the morning and the other started at the
New pool and then went on down to the Clachoil. We would
change beats after lunch.

On this particular day we arrived at the fishing hut opposite the
Deer Fence pool to find that both turbines were running and the
river was very high indeed. Bob was rather disappointed at this as
he hoped that we would have been able to catch it just before the
rise began, at a time when fish very often took as they felt the
influx of fresh water. The Deer Fence pool was so high that only
the glide opposite and below the hut remained fishable, but while
we were putting up our rods I noticed a fish head and tail close to
the bank on the edge of the current. I hurriedly finished tying on a
1/0 Garry Dog fly and, as Ian as usual was querying my choice of
fly, I pretended that I was concerned at his criticism and put out a
bit of line on the excuse that I wanted to see how it looked in the
water. Ian and Willie had won the toss and had chosen to start
fishing on the Deer Fence pool and poaching their water, I carefully cast over the fish I had seen move. First cast he had it and I
duly landed a nice ten pound fish covered with sea lice. So in the
face of hurt abuse and accusations of poaching their water, Bob
and I collected the rest of our tackle and walked on down to the
New pool to start fishing our beat.

This was in splendid order, especially the quiet smooth tail, but
we neither caught nor moved anything, nor did we see a fish move

although we covered the pool with several flies. It was the same story when we tried Clachoil where we spent the rest of the morning and the Fairburn side faired no better even from the boat. They had caught just one fish there earlier in the morning just as the river was rising.

At lunch we made our way back upstream to the hut where we found Ian spinning the New pool whilst Willie watched from the bank. We learned that they had not even seen a fish after we left, and Ian was still pulling my leg about catching the one and only fish in his pool when he stopped fishing to show me his new spinning reel. Out of interest I picked it up and having been shown how to work it, threw a long square cast out into the New pool and began to wind it in slowly. To my amazement a fish took the first cast, a model of a fish, short and thick weighing thirteen pounds and covered with sea lice. This, of course, made the day for Bob and me and provided us with an ideal opportunity to pull the other couple's legs unmercifully. We did so in spite of the fact that all four of us knew that it was an absolute fluke that my minnow had crossed the path of a taking fish at exactly that moment.

After lunch we swapped beats and fished hard all afternoon, but to no avail. The water looked promising but no fish moved to anything at all. About four o'clock in the afternoon the turbines were switched off as the Hydro Board stopped generating and the river then began to drop quickly. At last we had renewed hopes as the shape of the pools now became more clearly defined, and at the same time much more water became fishable. The Deer Fence pool and the runs below it were absolutely perfect and as we fished them down I certainly expected to catch a fish almost every cast, especially as the fish themselves became more active and moved freely for the first time that day.

Try as we might, however, the fish remained uninterested and, although we bided our time and fished well on into the evening expecting them to settle after an hour or two, our luck never changed. The other couple came up and joined us and had exactly the same story to recount, having seen masses of fish but found no takers amongst them.

Bob was very disappointed at this as he had hoped that we would have had a really good day for theoretically everything should have been in our favour, but we were all far to experienced fishermen to be in the least bit worried and everyone had enjoyed the day immensely.

Willie and I packed up our gear and departed for home while Bob and Ian went back to Marybank to have some supper, planning to return to the river about eight in the evening and fish on till dusk, hoping by then that the fish would have settled after the rise and fall in water height and therefore be in a better frame of mind to take. I phoned Bob later in the week to find out how they had got on, only to be told that try as they might they couldn't even move a fish that evening, but the following day he and another friend of his had caught fourteen grilse, most of them taken in the Deer Fence pool and the runs below it. This just goes to show how easily fish can be put off the take by a sudden alteration of water height. The day before we had fished, eleven salmon and grilse had been caught on the Coul beat and certainly it was the stiffest day I have ever experienced on that fascinating piece of water for when the grilse are running, a good bag is normally guaranteed.

This shows clearly one of the worst effects of Hydro schemes from the angler's point of view, and in the chapter on the Shin I have shown how the pattern of fishing on this famous river has changed for all time. The Shin Hydro Scheme involved the construction of two dams at Lairg. The water from the lower diversion dam is fed to the generating station upstream of the mouth of the river by means of a long tunnel running parallel to the left bank of the river, and is then returned to the natural course of the river just above its mouth. The provision for compensation flow conditions on the Shin now means that during the fishing season the river flows at a low/medium height and never varies as it would under natural conditions, unless freshets are released from the dam. In the spring it is always lower and in the summer it is generally higher, therefore, than natural flow. This has affected the behaviour of the spring run; fish pass arrangements have affected the natural spawning potential of the head water in the burns at the head of Loch Shin and the scheme has altered the Shin from being a spring river to a river where the main run is now in the summer and autumn. That is the inevitable result of all hydro constructions of that type and I know of no scheme of this sort that has not had a similar effect.

On the Conon the arrangement is quite different. There, generation takes place at the Torachilty dam at the top of the Coul water and in addition to the normal compensation flow which provides low to medium-low conditions for the whole of the river below the dam, the river is also subject to instantaneous floods whenever generation of electricity takes place. On these rivers the rise immediately below the dam is almost instantaneous and when both turbines are switched on together the river can go up by three to four feet in as many minutes. Even further downstream the increase in water height will only last for around fifteen minutes as it has to fill the various nooks and crannies in the configuration of the course of the river, while if such a rise occurred in nature as a result of rain it would only take place over several hours.

Similarly, the river will hold this height as long as generation of electricity is taking place and it then drops like a stone immediately the turbines are switched off.

On that day in July, many years ago, we suffered from an exaggerated instance of what can happen on these rivers when such a rise in the water takes place.

All fishermen know that salmon are very sensitive in their taking habits and one of the worst fishing conditions you can have is unsettled water accompanied by a rising river. Just occasionally, even at the height of the grilse run, these circumstances created by generation can cause the fish to go completely off the take. This happened on that day.

Coracles

It is many years since I fished from a coracle and there must be few men alive now who fully understand the art of building and handling them, but what a delight they were and how much I regret their passing. For there are rivers and beats on rivers where the coracle is really irreplaceable and I am sure that the annual catch on such beats will have declined as a result.

Soon there may be few left indeed who have had experience of fishing from a coracle and so, for those who do not know, I will chronicle this art as it was practised before the war.

A coracle is basically the frame of a large wickerwork basket covered with canvas and waterproofed with pitch. It is a descendant of the primitive craft of prehistoric man when such boats were covered with animal hides. Coracles are roughly square in shape and are of various sizes and designs, generally they take either one or two men. They have a seat which runs along the middle and in a two man coracle the handler and the fisherman sit side by side. They are propelled by a flat bladed paddle and in water less than four feet deep the handler holds the coracle in position with a seven foot spiked iron staff.

Coracles are so light that they can be carried on a man's back for a considerable distance and this was the practice on beats of the Welsh Dee where coracles were in common use. They were and are virtually impossible to propel upstream except in the slackest water because their shape tends to make them spin round and round save when they are in the hands of a real expert. But they are very manoeuvrable down and across stream, and as they have no keel of any sort they create far less disturbance on the water than an ordinary boat, and in the hands of an expert can be shot down quite tumultuous rapids very easily.

Much of my father's water on the Welsh Dee was ideally suited to fishing from a coracle for two reasons. The first was that, like much of the Dee, the banks were heavily lined with trees and the pools too deep to wade. It was therefore impossible to fish them properly with a fly unless you got out into the water, as the trees stopped you casting and the pool could then only be fished either with a minnow or bait, neither of which were so satisfactory. The other factor was that on many pools a rock ledge ran down the entire length. This ledge was usually just under water when the river was low and thus, at most heights of water, it was relatively easy to wade along it and fish the pool. However, this never produced a satisfactory result. Occasionally when fishing with a fly from the ledge you caught a fish in the deeper water, but I am sure that the vibration of the angler walking along this ledge drove the fish from their lies, which often were in the deep water just at the edge of the ledge and this vibration, of course, did not take place when the pool was fished from the coracle. I think this often happens in rocky gorgy pools and I have proved it to myself time and time again by fishing a pool blank from the ledge and then catching a fish immediately afterwards fishing the pool from a coracle.

It was the top of our beat that we normally fished with the coracle. And it was Robert Jones who handled the coracle for us. Robert was a wonderful old Welshman, a master craftsman at many different trades, dry stone dyking, woodcutting, slitting logs for fencing, he also made his own coracles and there were few who could handle one better. I can see him still in my imagination, a man of fity or so, trim and neat of medium build with a grey moustache. He was always immaculately dressed in a heavy tweed jacket with waistcoat, out of which hung the chain of his fob watch. He wore well cut corduroy breeches, pinkish brown in colour, with leather gaiters and highly polished black hobnailed boots and the whole was surmounted by a green or brown felt trilby hat, the band of which was often adorned by several favoured fishing flies.

Robert was immensely knowledgeable about fishing and shooting. He had eyes like a hawk and could always tell when a fish had come to the angler's fly twenty yards away, even if that fish made no visible mark or blemish on the surface of the river. When we arranged to go fishing he was always waiting for us by the seat in front of the summer-house at the bottom of the steps which led down from the house with his seven foot long gaff and rubber-lined carpenter's bag which he used for carrying the fish, beside him. He would have my father's rod all ready for him with the gut cast soaking just off the breakwater while upstream the coracle lay waiting, resting four feet off the ground on its wooden platform with the paddle and staff beside it.

I remember one evening in April when my father came home from work. The late Duke of Westminster's party had permission to fish the Summer-house pool and so my father decided that he would go to the top of the water to fish the Pentre pool from the coracle. I went with him with my trout rod as there was only room for one person to fish from the coracle at a time.

It was a perfect evening for fishing with the river at an ideal height. My father had on his favourite 2/0 Silver Wilkinson and he and Robert embarked in the coracle at the top of the Pentre pool. I went to fish the runs above, between the Pentre and Mill pool for trout. I watched them push out some distance from the bank to fish the 'Double-stone' lie in the centre of the river almost opposite the launching place. As they covered this lie I saw two fish move lower down the pool. Robert worked the coracle in against our bank to float over the ledge and soon afterwards when they reached the 'Five Trees' lie I saw my father's line tighten and he was into a fish. After a short battle a gleaming thirteen pound salmon lay on the bottom of the coracle and Robert pulled the coracle several yards upstream so that they could fish down over the lie again. Within minutes another fish was being played, a smaller one which pulled the balance down to ten pounds.

I stopped fishing and came down to watch them, sitting on the bank high above as they fished down the tail of the pool. At that height of water a fish could lie almost anywhere down its length but nothing moved in several of the favoured places. Then as they came to the best lie in the pool I could see that Robert was full of hope. He let the coracle down barely a yard at a time and just off the ledge, opposite a grassy clump, his patience was rewarded as first my father caught a fifteen and a half pound salmon, and then just as dusk was falling a last fish, rather larger than the rest at seventeen pounds.

As I walked down the path to the summer-house I saw the coracle shooting the rapids, Robert deftly steering between the rocks and when I reached the landing place they had already come ashore. It had been a memorable evening and as the last glimmer of daylight faded from the sky we stowed the coracle away. Robert put the fish in his converted carpenter's bag and we all climbed the steps to the house.

I remember another occasion when we fished the Pentre pool from the coracle. It was in 1939 and for several days after the opening of the season the river had been too high to make the Pentre pool worth fishing. Then it began to drop and that afternoon I set off with my mother, who was also a keen angler, just after lunch. Robert met us at the usual place and suggested that we went up to the Pentre pool and left the Summer-house pool for my father to fish on his return from work. This we did. My mother fished down first and although several fish moved to her fly none took solidly. Half way down the pool we swopped places but the same thing happened to me, fish moved to several different flies but none of them took solidly. On our way down Robert suggested that we fish the Willow pool, and again we moved some fish but nothing more. When we met my father he explained that this behaviour was not uncommon when salmon had newly arrived in a pool but had not yet settled properly in their lies. In my short fishing experiences at that time I found this very difficult to understand but my father assured me that as the river dropped the fish would start to take properly, and he was quite right for we caught no fewer than twenty-three fish in the next three days, including one of twenty-nine pounds caught by Lady Mary Grosvenor.

My own first fish from the coracle was a memorable occasion. Robert was attending the Duke of Westminster's party on the Summer-house beat but that morning he had carried the coracle up to the Pentre pool in case we wanted to fish that beat. My father was a good coracle handler and was keen that I should learn how to handle one for myself, and he also wanted me to catch a fish from one. After lunch we set sail at the head of the pool with my father handling the paddle and when we reached the 'Five Trees' lie I moved a fish three times to my fly which was a 3/0 Poynder. My father then told me to change my fly to one slightly smaller and I reeled in and tied on a 2/0 Silver Wilkinson in a fever of excitement. Next cast I hooked the fish and after a number of exciting incidents it was safely landed.

I then persuaded my father to let me handle the coracle so that he could fish out the rest of the pool. He was a bit reluctant to do this but I promised that if I got into difficulties I would hand him the paddle and take the rod. However, I managed to let the coracle down the next thirty yards of the pool in fair style and as we got to the best lie in the pool my father's line tightened and he was into a fish. Immediately I swung my legs over the side, and

River Eden – Cumbria.
Typical Coracle water.

having got a good foothold on the ledge held the coracle steady while he played the fish. Much to my relief, as the fish started to get tired Robert arrived and came down the bank and gaffed it. It was a beauty of twenty-five and a half pounds, one of those fish that you dream about.

During the war our water at Argoed was only fished occasionally, and Robert Jones died shortly after the end of the war. From then on we had no-one who could handle a coracle properly as my father was by then too old and our catches from the Pentre pool declined radically; I think this is a common experience on many of the best beats of rivers which were formerly fished from a coracle.

The only exception to this was when a friend of mine, Edwin Hill Trevor, came to fish with us. He brought with him a miner called Evans who was an expert coracle man. I remember two days with Evans when the Pentre pool was in order. On the first, my father caught three salmon in an afternoon, twenty-four, nineteen and seventeen and a half pounds, and on another Saturday I caught four fish and lost another. We never caught as many when fishing from the bank.

No chapter on the coracle would be complete without a mention of the late Captain Hughes Parry who fished on the Feachan water of the Welsh Dee, just below Llangollen. This beat contained the famous Slaughterhouse pool which was one of the most productive on the whole of the Dee. Captain Hughes Parry had a legendary reputation both as an angler and a coracle man and was often seen fishing his water alone in a small one man coracle. He had no difficulty, even in the heaviest water, in handling his coracle and fishing and when he hooked even a heavy fish he was able to bring things to a successful conclusion.

Vibration

Vibration is a far more important factor in fishing than most people realise and I would say that all anglers in the course of their fishing life have caused disturbance this way and probably blamed something else when the damage was done. Vibration affects some pools, beats or rivers worse than others. Those rivers that have gravelly banks or run through loam are little affected. Others, particularly those with rock edges, cliffs or buttresses are affected much more and the worst of all are pools where rocky shelves project from the bank well out into the pool, especially when these ledges are undermined. This is because fish very often lie tight in beside these shelves or even underneath them, and therefore they are peculiarly sensitive to waves of vibration transmitted through the seams of the rock.

All fishermen should avoid careless heavy movements in their approach to pools that have rocky outcrops protruding out into the water and this is so at any height of river, although this effect is exaggerated in low water flow and drought conditions. Anglers should also try and avoid standing on ledges or rock shelves that run out into the pool, particularly if there is an alternative stance, and this is one of the main reasons why fishing from a coracle on the Welsh Dee was so much more effective than wading down the rock ledges that ran out into the pool.

Another factor that many anglers do not realise is the effect of a dog on the river bank. Dogs are great companions but it is very important that if you go fishing with a dog you do not let it scamper up and down the banks in an uncontrollable way. Very often the quick darting action of a dog can be seen by fish while at other times the pitter patter of a dog's feet on rock ledges and shelves is transmitted through the pools, and this can cause sufficient disturbance to shift a taking fish out of its lie.

I remember the first time that I noticed a definite disturbance by

117

dogs. I was sitting one Sunday afternoon in a wood at the Major pool on the Dee, on top of a cliff in the shade of an oak tree looking at seventeen salmon lying beside the rock face just below where I sat. I was waiting for a fishing friend of my father's to return from his lunch, as he was planning to try to catch one of these fish with a prawn. After about half an hour I suddenly saw one or two of the fish starting to get restless, and then all of a sudden all the fish disappeared from the lie into the deeper water of the pool. I looked around and I saw that my sister's two dachsunds and her deerhound were bounding towards me. I was amazed at this as I could not really believe that these dogs had caused enough disturbance to move the salmon, so after some discussion I persuaded Rosemary to tie her dogs up to a fence some two hundred yards away from the river. We then sat down beside the tree and watched the underwater ledge hoping the fish would return and sure enough, one by one, they returned from the depths and took up residence beside the cliff face. After ten minutes, fifteen of the seventeen salmon were lying peacefully there once again.

As there was no sign of my father's friend I asked Rosemary to walk quietly away and release her dogs, to see whether the fish were again disturbed by the dogs running to me. There was absolutely no movement as she quietly left the scene, but as soon as she released the dogs and I had called them to me the fish again immediately disappeared into the depths of the river.

There is no doubt in my mind, having seen this type of incident happen on numerous occasions and on several rivers, that it is the quick pitter-patter movement of the dog and not the deliberate, quiet approach of a human being that causes the disturbance and vibration that fish dislike and fear. I can only assume that the vibration pattern is similar to that made by an otter or another predator and I would say that on this occasion and on others there was no question at all of the fish seeing the dogs as they were completely unsighted from the river.

There are two other types of vibration which I have noted during my years as a fisherman. The first of these is mechanical vibration and the second is that caused by low flying aircraft.

The first time I noticed the disturbance caused by mechanical vibration occurred once again on the Welsh Dee. The main pool on the beat, the Summer-house pool, was a long streamy pool with a man-made breakwater running on top of a rock foundation on

The Crows Nest – River Cassley.
A typical gorge pool fished from the ledge by the tree stump.

the right bank and a sixteen acre arable field lying twenty yards back from the left bank of the river. Between the river and this field there was a fringe of gravel and willow trees lying on top of a rock shelf.

When I was a boy my father's farm tenant used to work the farm on the left bank with eight pairs of horses and I can still remember the magnificent sight of those teams of horses marching up and down those fields as their drovers methodically ploughed and tilled them. However, just before the last war the farmer bought his first tractor and from then on the horses gradually disappeared. Early in the war I came home from school one April and immediately rushed straight down to the river to fish. It was late afternoon and naturally I started at the Summer-house pool. The river was in perfect order, but to my great disappointment by the time I had fished to the end of the pool I had moved nothing to my fly. I was sitting on the breakwater changing my fly when Robert Jones, who had now partially retired, appeared. He gave me a great welcome and then said in his broad Welsh accent 'I'm afraid you're wasting your time fishing here, there is a tractor working in the bottom of the sixteen acre. You had better fish the Major till he leaves, he won't be long, he's nearly finished his work.'

I was perplexed by this time but he was so adamant that I decided it was best not to argue, but I resolved to discuss it with my father later in the evening.

Robert went with me down to the Major pool and having checked the fly I had been fishing with advised me to leave it on. I fished the short stream carefully and almost on my last cast a fish took my fly solidly. After a short sharp struggle, Robert gaffed it expertly under the chin, a fresh gleaming spring fish of just under ten pounds.

Although we could now no longer hear the noise of the tractor coming across the river, Robert waited before suggesting we return to the Summer-house pool. He made me fish the Major again and then took me up to the Run, a pool lying midway between the Major and the Summer-house pool. I fished this carefully, but again with no result and then at last we returned to the head of the Summer-house pool. Robert gave me a bright smile and said quietly 'We will get one now the tractor is away'. Sure enough I got a fish high up in the stream, and then having been joined by my father I caught a second low down near the lone tree.

When I discussed Robert's remarks about the tractor with my father later in the evening he explained that the Summer-house pool had become far more temperamental in recent years for no apparent reason and on many occasions, even during the 1939 season which was one of the best years we have ever had with the river in perfect order for week after week, this pool, which seemed certain to yield a fish, was blank for a good deal of the time. Both my father and Robert Jones had thought very carefully about this apparent change in the taking habits of salmon, as normally the Summer-house pool was the most reliable free taking pool on our beat whenever it was in order, and one day Robert had suggested his theory about a tractor working in the field on the opposite bank. Although my father initially doubted whether this solution was correct, he carefully noted the details of the non-taking times and the tractor working in the field and eventually concluded that this was correct and this was the reason for the fish not taking.

For many years afterwards I tried to disprove this theory but there is no doubt that once the river dropped to medium height it was practically useless to fish this pool with anything but a bait, and only then in the deep water areas, when a tractor was working in the field opposite. As soon as the tractor stopped, after a short time the fish would return to the shallower lies in the pool and begin to take the fly again.

The other aspect of vibration is that caused by low flying air-craft. As I live in an area where low flying is permitted, I have had ample opportunity to observe fish behaviour when aircraft pass directly overhead. It is quite often possible to feel the vibration oneself as an aeroplane passes and, as soon as it is past, I have seen fish that formerly were lying high in the water either give a quick movement or merge perceptibly lower. If you are unfortunate and suffer from one of those days where the aeroplanes are perpetually chasing each other around the mountains in the North of Scotland, I would think that you are well advised to try and find pools on your beat that have gravelly bottoms, as I have observed that it is only pools with rocky outcrops that actually transmit this vibration to the fish lying close to them.

A Day on Loch Stack

I suppose that everyone who has fished a lot from a boat on a Loch has had the galling experience of watching his companion catch fish after fish and himself remain quite out of luck. I have been on the receiving end of this on many occasions and have observed that when the gods are looking favourably on one rod than the other no action seems to make the slightest difference. I have seen ghillies turn the boat round, anglers change rods, anglers fish with exactly the same flies, but if that is the way the fates have decided on that particular day nothing really makes any difference.

In the summer of 1959 I had one of the most embarrassing day's fishing of my life with a very old friend George Baxter, who was a fellow Fishery Consultant. He was a very keen sea trout fisher and fished a lot on Loch Maree. As he was coming up to Sutherland he asked me whether I could arrange a day's fishing for him and his wife on Loch Stack, the famous sea trout loch on the west coast of Scotland, and this I did. On 17th July we motored over from Invershin in the morning so that we could start fishing at ten a.m. I had booked a boat at Ardhuillen, the east end of the loch, and our ghillie was to be Willie Elliott, son of the head ghillie of the loch, who was young, strong, and keen as mustard. It was a bright sunny day in the middle of one of the finest summers this century and there was a very gentle wind blowing from the east which made the smallest ripple on the water. There wasn't anything like enough wind to fish the dap and there wasn't enough to enable you to trip your bob fly on the top of the water. This was a pity as George's wife only dapped and I prefer bobbing my fly on the top of the wave when loch fishing if I can. However, this was not to be, and we started fishing with ordinary wet flies. I had on a floating line with a cast of three flies, a Black Pennel in the bob position, a Grouse and Claret in the centre and a Peter Ross as my tail fly. George was using an ungreased Kingfisher line and three flies of his own choice.

The day was so still and bright with only a few thin wisps of cloud to cover the sun that I was not at all hopeful, but immediately we started our first drift on the Table Bank just outside the narrows I felt a light pull and I hooked a nice sea trout which weighed just under two pounds. This fish had taken the Black Pennel and I then caught another, a little bit smaller, on the same fly. George had moved a fish or two, but he had not made contact with anything. We finished off the Table Bank drift and then moved over to the Ardnahuillen shore to fish Red Rock. I caught two more fish on my Black Pennel while George caught one and when we had finished that drift and were rowing across to Island Bank I wound in my line and changed the Peter Ross for another Black Pennel in the tail position. It seemed to me that I had not moved a fish to either of the other two flies I had on, and I might as well put an additional Black Pennel on my cast as that was the fly the fish seemed to be taking.

I caught another fish at Island Bank and then we went on to Sandy Bay and a drift between the points where I caught several fish, one after the other, all on the Black Pennel. This was now rather embarrassing. George was hardly moving a fish and he refused to accept any of my pattern of Black Pennel which was proving so successful. In spite of changing the boat round to reverse our fishing positions, nothing seemed to make any difference. At lunch we had fifteen fish in the boat of which I had caught all but two.

While we were having lunch the wind began to strengthen a bit from the east. Immediately he saw this Willie suggested that we should try the Blackstone Bank after lunch with one wet fly rod and the dap. When we had finished there we would then go on to deeper water over towards the road in case the dap was successful in raising some of the bigger fish. He also urged us not to linger over lunch in case the wind should drop as quickly as it had got up. George's wife got out the dapping rod, but my friend, who was an elderly man, said that he would take a rest and made me go on fishing. I now changed my grouse and Claret for a Black Pennel as all the fish I had caught in the morning had taken this fly either in the bob or the tail position, and I thought that I might as well fish with three flies of the same pattern.

We then started the long drift on the Island bank down to the Blackstone Bank and while some fish moved to the dap, my friend's wife touched nothing while I continued to pick up the odd fish. After that we rowed to the deep water by the road where I thought that the fortunes were bound to change as I would be most unlikely to catch anything there on the wet fly, but shortly after I had started fishing I caught a beaufiul sea trout of six and a half pounds. As I was playing this fish the wind started to die away and my friend's wife had to take down the dapping rod. We then returned to the best banks for the wet fly and at last my friend started to catch the odd fish and we ended the day with twenty-seven in the boat weighing sixty pounds in all. A really magnificent basket.

Although there is no doubt that on that particular day my luck was in while George Baxter's was out, I do think the reason I was successful on that particular day, while he was not, is quite easy to understand. I was fishing with a floating line and therefore I had to work my flies slowly and gently in the slight ripple to avoid making any disturbance on the surface. At the same time my flies were high in the water. George was fishing with a sinking line and moving his flies quite fast so that they would not sink too deep in the water. I am sure that it was the difference of presentation that made all the difference.

Actually, after many years experience and reflection I think that the conditions on that day while on the face of it appeared hopeless, were in fact extremely good. In my experience the one thing that you need for sea trout fishing on a loch is a constant wind. It doesn't have to be very strong but it is very important that it continues to flow throughout the day from the same direction. On that day the wind came lightly but definitely from the east and there was a gentle ripple. An east wind, in fact, rather suits Loch Stack because it does not buffet off the surrounding hills, and the size of the ripple is not really very important apart from preventing the use of the dap. This is quite different from salmon fishing in a loch where you need as big a wave as you can get, and if there are troughs in the waves so much the better. Even when the wind strengthened after lunch that day it blew constantly from the same direction, and there were never any skuds or cat's paws blowing across the surface of the water. Also, while the day was bright and sunny, there were fine wisps of cloud which came across the face of the sun from time to time. This took the glare from the water although I have found that sun makes little or no difference when I am sea trout fishing. Very often I have had a good bag in very sunny conditions.

I have noticed that if you are loch fishing on a day when there is very little wind, if the wind does not get up you very seldom have much success until it has settled into one quarter for half an hour or more. It seems to me that fish take at least that amount of time to become adjusted to the wind direction and come on to the take again.

I can remember another occasion fishing in very similar conditions with a very light east wind and bright sun on the Kyle of Sutherland. That day the wind was so light that it could not blow us upstream against the ebb tide and this meant that our boat was drifting down over the fish before they saw our flies. In spite of this we caught eleven sea trout in under two hours, averaging one and a half pounds in weight.

I think that all these things are of interest and when you are fishing in a boat with someone it often pays to look closely at the methods and presentation being used by your companions. This can make little difference to the result as we all know, but on that day I think that if George Baxter had greased his line or swapped rods he would have caught his share of the fish, and I only wish that he had done so.

Dapping

All my life I have been fascinated by the way that fish take the fly, and I have been extremely lucky as I have lived for many years on a river which has enabled me to observe salmon actually taking the fly. Such knowledge can help enormously in the way that an angler strikes the fish and the number of fish on the bank at the end of the day.

One of the most difficult fish of all to hook is the fish that takes the dapped fly on the loch, especially the sea trout which often comes at the fly with such a wallop that the fisherman is startled out of his wits and strikes far too soon. We have all done it, and I would say that all fishermen who in the future fish with a dap, will do so too.

However, while I cannot produce any easy panacea which will enable more fish that are risen to the dapped fly to be hooked, I once had a most interesting and unusual experience which, if I am right, would mean that more fishermen would fish with the dap than do and the total fish in a boat at the end of the day would be more. I don't assert this as a definite hypothesis, because my experience was unique, but I do think it may contain pointers that we would all do well to heed.

Some years ago I rented the stalking in a nearby forest in September. The day was hot, almost unbearably so, without a breath of wind. Sandy, the stalker, and I were high up on the hill waiting for the deer to settle below us. At our feet was a narrow Highland loch, typical of many of those found in the mountainous terrain. That day, some thirty feet below us the surface of the loch was glassy still and we could see right down into its depths and almost count the stones on its bottom. It was not a loch of any particular note; it had no reputation for its trout and so far as we were aware was hardly ever fished. As I gazed down into its depths I saw what at first I took to be some very narrow dark stones, and as I continued to look one or two of these 'stones' moved slightly and I became aware that I was seeing trout. And these were not just ordinary trout: they were certainly between one and four pounds in weight and a number of them may well have been larger.

Sandy, who was also a keen fisherman, and I discussed these fish and we decided that the next day that the wind was suitable for us to stalk this beat we would bring a trout rod with us to see if we could catch a fish or two. A few days later the wind was in the right quarter and we set off, loading the pony with my trout rods and tackle. I had decided that I would take both a dapping rod as well as a normal wet fly rod and that I would dap if I could, for I thought that this would be the best chance of catching one of the larger trout we had seen.

It was a lucky day. By twelve o'clock I had shot two good stags just beyond the loch and while they were being loaded on to the ponies I collected my tackle and set off to the loch. Unfortunately the wind had changed. Instead of blowing into the cliff from where we had seen the fish it was now blowing directly away from it. The only place where I had any chance of getting the dap to work was from the top of the cliff, and needless to say the water below the cliff was still and calm as it was sheltered from the breeze.

Nevertheless I resolved at least to try. The ripple started about twenty yards out from my shore and looking down into the water I could see no sign of the trout we had seen on our previous visit. However I climbed the cliff, put up my rod, tied on a medium-sized black and brown dapping fly, and even prospected for a good path down to the water's edge in case I should hook a fish. When I started fishing I found that the wind took my line out quite nicely for about fifteen yards from the shore where the fly worked well, but this was over the calm still water and I could not get the fly out over the ripple some five yards further out. As I could clearly see down into the water and there were no fish anywhere near the fly I thought that I was on a losing wicket. I was just about to abandon the dap and take to the wet fly when I saw a shape emerge from the ripple and make its way slowly towards my fly. Shaking with excitement I started to tell myself not to strike too soon, but to my dismay the fish made no attempt to take the fly but merely circled round beneath it, keeping probably about two inches beneath the surface without making any attempt to take it.

The trout continued to swim around just under the fly for what seemed at the time to be an age but probably was no more than a few minutes, and then I saw one shadow and then another emerge from the ripple and join the first fish, all of them swimming in the same direction clockwise at varying depths below the fly. After a bit I could count no fewer than seven fish below the fly, one of which was much larger that the others. At this point the wind strengthened and my fly began to snake more violently in jerks over the water. Immediately one of the trout, not the very big one, came up and took the fly.

Luckily I managed to hook it and after a short fight I swung a lovely fish up on to the gravelly beach, just under two pounds. When I had killed the fish and covered it with sphagnum moss, I climbed the cliff again and sat down to eat a sandwich and dry my fly. When I had hooked the fish the other trout had mostly disappeared straightaway, save for two which had swum round close to the hooked fish while it was being played with no apparent fear or alarm, but when I landed the fish they also had vanished.

I then let my dap go again, and believe it or not the whole episode was repeated three times in the course of the afternoon. During the afternoon several fish came to the fly which either were missed by me or did not take the fly properly. The final bag was four fish: three pounds two ounces, one pound thirteen ounces and two just over a pound.

I had often dapped before, both for brown and sea trout, and until that afternoon I had not really made up my mind why the dap attracted as it did, and also how fish came to the dap. What I did know was firstly, that dapping tended to attract the larger fish in a loch; secondly, you could dap with success on the deeper parts of the loch; and thirdly, that providing conditions allowed it was advantageous, if two rods were fishing from a boat, for one of them to fish with a traditional wet fly and for the second rod to dap. When this took place I had observed that the total catch for the boat was usually unequally divided. When it was relatively calm then it seemed to me that the wet fly caught the lion's share but when it was gustier and the dap jerked more erratically over the surface then the dapping rod was the more successful – certainly in raising fish, though fish that come to the dap are notoriously hard to hook, either because they miss the fly themselves or because the angler misses them.

On the day that I have described there was quite enough wind for the dap to work quite well on the smooth surface of the water and I would say that the dap was out and working for about fifteen minutes before the first fish appeared. It was interesting to note that there was no urgency about the movement of this fish towards the fly, nor for that matter was there any urgency about any of the other fish that came and circled underneath it. Only when a sharp gust of wind made the dap move sharply did the fish appear to hesitate and begin to move quickly, only for the slow, regular circling pattern to be resumed when the dap steadied down again.

The other six fish that came to the dap on the first occasion then came at fairly regular intervals, with probably no more than a minute between each appearance. When the dap began to jerk violently the fish that took it moved like lightning and slashed at the fly on the surface. Some of the other fish that were underneath the fly moved to it at the same time.

After I had landed the first fish there was never the same delay before the next trout appeared beneath it, although the time between the actual takes varied between ten minutes and half an hour.

On that day, certainly, the fish did not emerge from the depths of the loch and grab the fly. On the contrary they were drawn to the dap from a considerable distance and their approach to the fly was one of extreme caution except when the more erratic movement of the fly tempted them into taking it. This was on a loch which was virtually never fished and therefore the fish had no reason to be shy or wary. The more I think of this, and the more I consider this in the light of all the experience I have of fishing with the dap, the more I believe that this is the common behaviour of fish under normal circumstances.

Very often I have been in a boat fishing with a friend, both fishing with the traditional wet fly, and after a blank period one or the other of us has decided to put out a dap. Then very frequently after a period of ten to fifteen minutes that day has livened up and one or other of us has started to move fish. On some days both rods will move fish and on others only the wet fly. Before my experience I had assumed that we had met with a shoal of taking fish who happened to fancy the wet fly on that day. Now I think that these fish are very likely to have been drawn to the dap and while they may not take it they have taken the wet fly instead. But I think it was the dap which brought them to the vicinity of the boat in the first place, and if I am right then more loch and lake trout would be caught if more people dapped.

Eel Fishing

I will always remember a week on the Argoed water of the Welsh Dee in June 1948 when conditions for salmon fishing were just about as bad as they could possibly be. The river was dead low and had been low for some time. There was green algae on the rocks and river bed and the weather was warm, sultry, and thundery with only the occasional blink of sunshine breaking through the cloud cover. There were quite a number of fish in the river and these were now tucked in the shaded lies at the tails of the main holding pools. These fish were stale, lethargic and had seen every lure in the angler's book.

On Monday morning I went down to the river shortly after eight o'clock and met the old Welsh ghillie called Neron who often accompanied me when I was at home. I could see by the expression on his wizened face that he was resigned to another fruitless day on the river bank. He was, needless to say, quite right. I caught nothing all day, mainly fishing with a floating prawn and the only interesting thing that I do remember was that I saw a large salmon rise and take a leaf off the surface of the water which it then ejected after holding it in his mouth for about five seconds. I tried to cast a leaf over it, but was unable to imitate the motion of a free floating leaf on the surface of the river. As I bade Neron goodnight he asked me if I would mind if he brought some worms with him tomorrow as he wanted to try and catch some eels when I was fishing.

The next morning the weather was even more sultry than before and we could hear thunder rumbling in the distance. I was very despondent about my chances of catching a fish, but when I met Neron at the foot of the steps leading down to the Summer-house pool to my surprise he had a broad grin on his face, and he told me that the weather conditions were not very good for my job but excellent for his. I fished down the Summer-house pool and while I was doing so saw Neron take a huge jars of worms out of the pocket

130

of his coat and a ball of hemp out of another pocket. Using a bait needle, I saw him thread the hemp through the body of worm after worm until quite literally he finished up with a very long chain of worms which he then rolled up into a large ball, like a ball of knitting wool. When I had finished fishing the Summer-house pool I suggested that we go down to the Major pool whereupon he went into the the fishing hut and to my astonishment came out with an umbrella, an old sack full of newspapers, a stout nut stick and a length of blind cord. He then picked up my tackle bag, put the gaff over his shoulders, put the ball of worms in the sack and followed me down the breakwater that ran the length of the Summer-house pool to the Major pool.

I started to fish at the head of the pool and Neron went down to a backwater where the bank had been scoured just before the fence into the oak wood. I was so intrigued by his performance that very soon I stopped fishing and watched as he set up his equipment. First of all he put up the umbrella and stuck the spike at the top of it into the ground a short distance back from the bank so that the inverted side of the umbrella faced upwards. With an old tin which he found by the riverside he proceeded to fill the umbrella with about two inches of water. He tied one end of the blind cord to the end of the stick and passed the other end through the ball of worms. After that he took a short piece of brass piping out of his pocket and attached it to the blind cord below the worms, securing it with a firm knot. He then went to the edge of the breakwater and tossed the ball of worms into the water and stuck the butt end of the stick firmly into the ground.

I thought that this would be the end of the preparation, but I was wrong. He went over to his sack and, having taken the newspapers out of it, he laid it flat on the ground beside the umbrella and then spread some newspapers from the bundle on top.

Neron then came over and sat on the bank beside me about twenty yards above the stick. We chatted for a while and then I noticed that the cord attached to the stick was beginning to jerk. When I pointed this out, he nonchalantly answered 'they's beginning to bite', but he took no more notice . After a bit longer, the stick itself began to jerk far more violently in the ground and at that point Neron got up and walked forward to pick it up. He did this very gently and lifted the ball of worms clear of the water. To my astonishment, instead of just one eel being attached there were at least a dozen and Neron very slowly swung the stick round until these eels were over the newspaper on top of the sack where he shook it violently and they all fell off on to the newspaper. Of course, as there were no hooks involved, the eels were attached by their teeth only, entangled in the hemp.

Strangely enough once the eels touched the newspaper they only wriggled for a moment before lying quite still. Neron then went back to the river's edge and threw his bait into the water, replacing the stick into the ground once more. He then returned to the sack on which the eels were lying. Holding this like a tray he moved over the the umbrella and emptied all the eels into it. The umbrella had been carefully placed so that it was shaded by the trees. This performance went on all day and at the end of it, when I returned to Neron, I found that the umbrella was by now almost half full.

I sat down and started to question him about his fishing method, and first of all asked him why he had known so early in the morning that the conditions would be good for eel fishing. He explained that when the river was low, eels normally fed at night, and most of them spent the daylight hours hidden under stones and in rock crevices. However, when thunder was rumbling in the sky the rocks under which the eels were hiding vibrated, and they would come out from their refuge and swim about and were, therefore, much more likely to be caught under these conditions. The next question I asked him was why he waited until so many eels were on the bait before he lifted it. He replied that the disturbance of a lot of eels working at food attracted others from their hideout, and if you lifted the bait when the first eel began to nibble it that would be wasted. Thirdly, I asked him why the eels lay so still so soon after they touched the newspaper. His reply to this was that the dry paper acted like blotting paper and absorbed the natural slime of the eels' skin whereupon they lost the ability to crawl on its surface. The final point he made was that the shape of the inverted umbrella made it impossible for eels to crawl out of, while the water in the bottom of it kept them alive and fresh.

We agreed to pack up and go home and Neron lifted his bait out of the water for the last time. Shaking the eels attached to the bait in with the others, he then threw what remained of his worms into the river, wound up the blind cord, burnt the remainder of his newspapers and then soaked his sack in the river. He asked me to hold the sack open while he carefully lifted the umbrella, tilted one end and emptied the catch into the sack, the neck of which he tied up tightly. Then putting his umbrella under his arm, the sack on his shoulder, he bid me goodnight and walked off through the oak wood to his home in Cefn Mawr.

We fished for eels every day that week and Neron was well pleased as he sold them for two shillings and ninepence per pound while I never got bite from a salmon, but I had the privilege of watching a master at work and I think that there are many useful lessons for all fishermen to be learned from Neron's approach.

The first and foremost lesson that all anglers should learn is that it pays to study the habits of your quarry whenever you have the opportunity to do so. This of course is not easy to do in high water. But there must be a few fishermen who have not fished in drought conditions when the river was so low that fishing was useless and the river bed a skeleton of stones and boulders. It is in these conditions that the fisherman has the opportunity to study the banks and bed of the river in detail, pinpointing the rocks and undulations on the bottom of the pools and marking the lies where fish are likely to be taking in different heights of water. In very low conditions anyone with the help of polaroid glasses can generally see fish in the main lies of the pool quite clearly. And it can be of enormous benefit to observe carefully where fish are lying and also whether they vary the position they hold in the pool according to the time of day. This is often the case and many anglers do not realise how much fish can move about the pool even in the lowest water. Generally, this is brought about by the angle of the sun and in hot, low water conditions fish can often vary their position as many as three times in a day.

In the early morning you will find them in the faster, shallower streams at the head of the pool. Then, when the sun rises in the sky, unless these runs happen to be very well shaded, the salmon usually fall back into the deeper parts of the pool and lie fairly deep down in the water where they can escape from the intense rays of the sun. When a pool is too shallow for them to do this they will change position several times, following the shaded areas as the sun moves round. Once again, in the evening as the sun starts to set, salmon will move back into the streamy heads of the pools and they may even move upstream a pool or two during the night. Even in the lowest water conditions, providing that the water temperature is over 52°F, grilse and small salmon often push on upstream a pool or two during most nights in the summer, and on occasions they can be seen forcing their way through shallows with their backs almost completely out of the water.

Sometimes during a prolonged drought, and I would say that this does depend on the type of river, you will find that salmon sink right back into the deep holding areas of a pool and never bother to move at all. When this happens I think they realise that there is no hope of pushing on upstream until the weather changes, and it seems to me that they are then resigned to remaining where they are and conserving their energies by moving as little as possible. In these conditions I have quite often seen that fish then move up to the head of the pool twenty-four hours or so before the drought breaks and it has always seemed that they have a sixth sense which tells them that rain is coming. These fish are not uncatchable; they can be taken on a prawn or shrimp where the use of these baits are permitted, but the fisherman must know precisely where in the pool they are lying.

The second main lesson that I think Neron's eel fishing expedition tells all anglers is that regardless of conditions it always pays to anticipate what tackle you are going to require. Neron knew exactly what he needed down to the last detail and I think this is something that more fishermen should pay attention to. Very often I have seen anglers caught out by a sudden change of conditions, and many have arrived on the bank only to find that some essential part of the equipment has been left at home. Not only is this very annoying, it can sometimes make the difference between success and a blank day, and it can also be costly if the item has to be replaced by an additional purchase. I think that everybody should check their tackle meticulously and, even more important, when you return from a fishing holiday, unpack everything carefully and put it away making a note there and then of what needs replacing, or in the case of rods, repairing.

The final lesson that I think Neron teaches all fishermen is the extreme care he took over the handling and caring for his catch. Neron never actually handled the eels at all and made certain that they were kept alive and fresh in water. At the end of the day he even went to the trouble of making sure that his sack was thoroughly soaked so that the eels would be kept moist during his short walk home before he sold them. I think it costs nothing for any fisherman, whenever he has landed a fish, to make certain that it is put away carefully in the shade in a bass, or covered with bracken fronds so that it reaches home in the best possible condition. I know that nowadays there are people who carry ice boxes in their cars and this is a really excellent idea.

Decline of Salmon Stocks in Scotland

It would be fair to say that salmon are one of Scotland's most valuable natural resources. And, if they are managed, protected and exploited correctly, they can make a very important contribution to the economy of rural areas within which salmon rivers lie.

The salmon fisheries industry first of all provides direct employment. Net fisheries provide full and part time employment both on the coast and within river estuaries, while rod fisheries and District Fishery Boards provide both full and part time employment on the rivers themselves, involving protection work, hatchery work and angling. This employment is often found in isolated areas where alternative work would be difficult or impossible to find.

Salmon fishing also attracts many tourists both from home and abroad to fish in Scotland throughout the entire salmon angling season which lasts from January to November. Although many anglers come to fish during the main tourist season, many others come to fish between January–April and September–November, both periods of the year which are outside the normal tourist season. This particular clientele allows many hotels situated in river valleys to open earlier in the year and close later, thereby extending the season appreciably. This in turn often allows these hotels to become viable commercial enterprises which otherwise would have been difficult. Again this longer hotel season provides many extra jobs and extends employment in this trade.

The industry also provides many ancillary jobs in other occupations. Among these are boat building, net making, fishing tackle makers, tackle shops and waterproof clothing manufactures and many other fields.

It is difficult to put an exact figure on the benefit derived from tourists attracted by salmon fishing but several estimates of this have been produced. These vary from between £60 million to £180 million per annum. As well as this direct benefit, anglers and their families spend a considerable amount of money in the locality of the rivers. This helps craft shops, local traders, garages, bed and breakfast houses, to name a few. It is often the case that salmon fishings are directly responsible for forming the backbone of both employment and trade in small communities in the close proximity of river systems.

Both the ownership rights of salmon fisheries and the law governing the administration of salmon fisheries differ in Scotland from the rest of the United Kingdom. For this reason anglers from the south of the border and from abroad who fish in Scotland for salmon often find it difficult to understand the various complexities of these and tend to criticise the management of Scottish salmon fisheries.

In Scotland both net and rod fisheries were given to individuals through the centuries by means of written Crown Grants. All private titles to salmon fishing from such grants must be based on deeds recorded in the Register of Sasines, Edinburgh. Both rod and net fisheries are therefore separate hereditable estates and, unlike trout fisheries, do not necessarily follow land ownership. They do however carry adequate rights of access over land adjoining these fisheries and also, having the superior fishing rights, the right to fish for other species of fish in these waters. Trout fishing ownership cannot be divorced from land ownership and this often leads to situations whereby trout fishings are owned jointly by two different owners: the owner of the bank of the river and also the owner of the salmon fishing as the latter is the owner of the superior fishing rights.

At the present time in Scotland most rod fisheries are either privately owned, or as a result of a recent innovation owned on a time-share basis. The Crown also own some rod fisheries. However, once again there is an anomaly to this and that is that if salmon fishings are opened up in waters where salmon have never populated the area before, these fishings automatically belong to the Crown and not to the landowner. For example, if formerly impassable falls are by-passed or eased to allow salmon stocks to ascend, these new upstream salmon fisheries automatically belong to the Crown and not to the riparian landowners who may have carried out these works. In the case of estuary and coastal netting rights at the mouths of rivers and in the sea, although some of these are privately owned, many more are owned by the Crown and these are often leased by the Crown to individuals or companies.

There are cases in Scotland where some net and rod fishings are owned by local authorities. These are, in the main, situated close to the mouth of the river. Both the towns of Perth and Inverness, for example, own appreciable salmon fishing rights.

In England and Wales, rod fisheries, although mainly privately owned, are normally under riparian ownership and are not a separate hereditable right. Net fisheries are publicly owned by local authorities and these authorities issue licences to local residents to operate differing types of nets in their river authority area. The number of net operators allowed in each area is controlled under Net Limitation Orders fixed by each authority.

Salmon fisheries in Scotland have been the subject of legislation since 1318, but the acts of 1862 and 1868 form the basis of Salmon Law today. The 1951 Act was limited in scope and largely an anti-poaching measure, it also deals with the weekly close time for nets and collection of statistics.

Under the Salmon Fisheries (Scotland) 1862 Act, Commissioners were appointed and amongst their duties they were asked to establish Salmon Fishery Districts. The Statute enacted that for each district there would be a Board, consisting of three upper and three lower proprietors with, as Chairman, the proprietor having the largest annual valuation. The remit given to the Board was to protect, preserve and improve fisheries in their district. The Salmon Fisheries (Scotland) Act 1868 contained further provisions for administration by District Boards and defined by schedule such matters as district boundaries, division between upper and lower proprietors, annual close times and estuary limits. In all one hundred and six districts were defined, but at the present time only some fifty-five of these have Boards. Powers and duties of District Boards were prescribed by sections of both Acts.

District Salmon Fishery Boards are statutory bodies and have power under the 1862 Act to impose a fishery assessment to finance the Board. This assessment is levied on the annual rateable value of the fishery as entered in the Valuation Roll. The Fishery Board fixes its rate of levy annually, according to the total amount of revenue required to meet its obligation. There is no doubt that this legislation has held Scottish salmon fisheries in good stead for nearly a hundred years. During that period Scottish salmon fisheries went from strength to strength whilst many other nations with Atlantic salmon stocks saw the species either become extinct or their stocks dwindle to a fraction of their former strength.

Our forebears had the foresight to realise that the most essential factor in salmon fisheries management is to strike the right balance between net cull, rod catch and spawning escapement. This they did through careful thought and consideration given when fixing the annual and weekly open and close time for both rod and net fisheries. It is interesting to note that in some years during the late 1950s and early 1960s Scotland's Atlantic salmon catch was the highest by any nation in the world.

The fact that both the upper and lower proprietors formed the composition of a District Board was undoubtedly another very strong advantage in this legislation, because this brought rodsmen and netsmen with intimate knowledge of the district together round a table, and gave both parties equal responsibility in the day to day administration of the river system. The main difference between salmon fishery legislation in Scotland and that in England and Wales is, that District Boards in Scotland are self-financing and solely responsible for salmon and sea trout stocks in the river systems. These Boards since 1954 have been ably assisted by Scottish Purification Boards and Authorities whose responsibility is the health and cleanliness of our river systems. In England and Wales, River Authorities are responsible, not only for fisheries, but also for water, sewage and land drainage matters. The fishery side is financed by rod and net licences for salmon and fresh water fish and subsidised through the local authority rating system. This vast difference between ownership rights and the law administering salmon fisheries in Scotland, compared with that prevailing in England and Wales, makes it virtually impossible for the entire United Kingdom to have a common salmon policy for administration of these fisheries.

The decline of salmon stocks over the last twenty years has become a major subject of controversy. Few days pass without articles concerning the plight of salmon appearing either in the national press or one or other of the sporting magazines. On the whole the angling press, practically without exception, put the blame firmly on the shoulders of the netsmen and make this sector of the industry the scapegoat, a reputation the legal tacksmen has lived with for centuries. Forgotten completely in the heat of the moment are:

a) The instability of both river flow regimes and river bed and bank regimes due to land development, drainage, and water abstraction schemes on river catchments.

b) The fact that the grey seal population around the United Kingdom shores has risen from 30,000 in the 1960s to 88,000 in 1985.

c) The increase in both netting for salmon on their feeding grounds and interceptory netting for salmon between their feeding grounds and their rivers of origin.

d) More sophisticated and deadly methods of poaching both in fresh water and at sea.

e) Outdated legislation which is unable to deal with the problems of the modern era.

f) The outbreak of UDN disease, which hit salmon stocks in this country in 1967 and is still affecting them.

There is absolutely no doubt that it is a combination of these problems and pressures on salmon stocks and not one single factor alone which is responsible for the present state of salmon stocks in Scotland.

At the outset it is worthwhile examining carefully the true position of salmon stocks in Scotland. With so many anglers interested in salmon fishing in this country the subject can be a very emotive one, and for that reason the rate of the decline of salmon stocks has tended to become over-exaggerated. In actual fact it is questionable whether the *overall* number of salmon entering our river systems over a twelve month period has declined appreciably in the past twenty years. What is quite unquestionable is that early runs of fish have declined drastically. Analysing some of the statistics of rod fisheries for the 1950–60 period against those of the same fishery in the 1980s, we find that in the earlier period between 60% and 70% of the annual catch were taken before the end of June with the rest of the catch between then and the end of the season, whereas in the 1980s, catch figures at the end of June in many cases are no more than 30% of the annual catch and in one or two cases under 20%. Unfortunately this type of drastic swing from early to late runs of fish is not isolated to one or two river systems but seems to be the pattern throughout Scotland. There seemed to be a slight revival of spring runs in 1978 and 1980 but this has not been maintained.

As a result of this those rivers that remain open to the end of October or longer do not show a marked decline in total annual catch figures. This does not, generally, apply to other rivers that close on the 30th September. There is no doubt that this tendency for fish to run later in the year means that rivers that do close on the

30th September are likely to have many fish entering their river systems after the net and rod season is closed. These fish are therefore not culled or exploited and this could well cause problems in future years.

Catch statistics released by Department of Agriculture and Fisheries over the past number of years definitely show a heavy decline in the number of salmon and grilse caught by all methods in Scotland, but when these figures are broken up into fixed engine, net and coble, and rod catches it is clearly shown that, whereas the two net catches have dropped by 25% or more over the period, rod catches show a very constant figure with even a slight increase. I am fully aware that it can be argued, quite rightly, that far more effort is put into rod fishing in the present era and therefore on that basis rod catches should be greater. However it must be remembered that since 1967, UDN disease has been present in our rivers and although this in no way affects net catches in the estuaries and on the coast it does have a very definite bearing on the taking habits of the salmon once they enter the rivers. This has lowered catches at certain periods of the year when signs of the disease are clearly visible as salmon with UDN in their system never take freely.

There is another factor which has a bearing on rod catches. An increase in grilse numbers generally adds little to the total rod catches. Grilse *seldom* take freely when they enter the river in the summer. In the same way an increase in rod numbers on a river does not necessarily mean a *pro rata* increase in catches. The salmon is a wary creature with completely unpredictable taking habits at the best of times and the slightest touch of disease, alteration of water and weather conditions and over-fishing can drastically alter their catchability.

In order to protect, maintain and improve salmon stocks in the river system in the present era both the owner of the salmon fishery and also the District Fishery Board are put to great expense. As far as the fishery owners are concerned, the main reason why so much salmon fishing in Scotland today is let to tenants is so that they can raise sufficient revenue from their fishings to pay for the employment of ghillies, local fishery rates, Fishery Board Assessment and river maintenance. Obviously with the recent failure of the spring run the amount of revenue that it is possible to raise from letting rod fishing early in the year is now beginning to show a decline. If this decline continues, the amount of money fishery owners have available to spend on protection and re-stocking programmes will also be reduced, to the detriment of the fishery concerned. At the same time the rateable value of the fisheries will be lowered as local authority rates are very much allied to the catch of the fishery. This would also apply to net fisheries whose catches have also suffered as a direct result of the decline in spring fish. District Fishery Boards will also, therefore, soon find that they are having to levy their assessment on a very much smaller total rateable value and will in the end find that it is difficult to raise the amount of money required to meet their obligations, from this source. Therefore, in all probability, they will have to lower their standard with regard to protection and improvements, to the detriment of salmon stocks in the district.

The perfect situation is when the rod and net catches show a nicely arched graph which picks up in the beginning of the season, holds a gradual curve for as many months as possible, and then falls away gradually at the end of the season. Unfortunately the present situation in Scotland shows a shallow rising graph until the end of June and then a very steep peak, falling away around September and October. This means that only about half the season is productive as far as revenue to the Board is concerned and this can weaken the whole structure of river management.

This point is reinforced if one studies the history of the District Fishery Boards since they were first constituted after the 1862 and 1868 Acts. Most of the fifty-five District Boards that exist at the present time are to be found on the longer river systems either on the east or south-west coasts of Scotland. These rivers, due to their length, can accommodate spring, summer, and autumn runs of fish. However, many Boards on the west and north-west coasts have lapsed over the years, mainly due to the lack of finance caused by the fact that in these areas the rivers are much shorter, and most of them can only accommodate one run of fish, the summer run. They therefore have a severely reduced period in which to produce revenue. In many cases this created financial problems which prevented the Boards from carrying out their obligations.

Unless something is done quickly to re-balance the runs of fish entering our main river systems in Scotland to their former status, there is no doubt that many of our main rivers will be faced with the same financial embarrassment as the smaller west coast Boards have already suffered.

In order to look at this possibility within its proper context I would like to turn to the conservation aspects of salmon. It is common knowledge that salmon are migratory fish which breed in fresh water, feed at sea and then return again to fresh water. Very briefly the life cycle is for the eggs to be laid six to nine inches down in the gravel between late October and the end of January. The incubation period of the egg varies according to the mean temperature it is subjected to, that is if it is subjected to a mean of 45°F, it hatches in approximately ninety days, whereas if it is subjected to a mean of 37°F it will not hatch for approximately one hundred and forty days. This is nature's way of ensuring that eggs that are laid in the colder, higher catchment areas of our river systems do not hatch out until there is food available to sustain the progeny. When the ova hatches several inches below the surface of the gravel the progeny is known as aelvin. This is a transparent little creature, under an inch in length, which has a yolk sack hanging to the underside of its gill casing. This sack is the food supply which sustains the little fish as it worms its way through the gravel, under which it is hatched, to the surface of the river bed. Once the yolk sack is absorbed the aelvin is known as a fry and then after it has grown further, a parr.

These little fish feed in fresh water for a period of one to four years before migrating to sea, but in this country two to three years is the norm. When the parr are ready to migrate the marks and spots on their skin become obliterated by a coating of silvery guanine. This is to protect their skin and scales from erosion by sea water during their sea life. These fish are now known as smolts and descend the river system between the months of March to June. Having entered the estuary they pause briefly to acclimatise themselves to their new environment before heading out to their feeding grounds far from our shores. When these fish mature they return to fresh water once again for the prime and sole purpose of regenerating the species. Those that return after spending one sea winter at sea are known as grilse and those that stay two or more winters at sea are known as salmon.

There are four main runs of salmon in the spring, summer, autumn, and winter although scientists of the present day make no distinction between the winter and spring runs, merely calling the former early spring fish. Each of these runs overlap the next, the spring run beginning in January, reaching crescendo in early April, and tailing away towards mid-May. This is overlapped by the summer run, beginning early in May, reaching a peak in early June, and falling away in August. This in turn is overlapped by the autumn

142

run which begins in late August, reaching a peak in mid-October, and tailing away through November. Finally the winter run starts in early October, reaching its peak in early December, and then overlapping with the spring run. Both the summer and autumn runs have a large grilse component included. Whereas early grilse in late May and early June can be as small as one and a half to three pounds, late summer specimens can be as heavy as eight or nine pounds and some autumn grilse can even be heavier, twelve to sixteen pounds.

It is also possible on rivers such as the Tay in late September to mid-October to catch two fish on the same day, both straight out of the sea with sea lice, one of which is due to spawn within a matter of weeks while the other will not spawn until the following autumn. This is a typical case of winter runs over-lapping the autumn runs.

A river system always gets stocked from top to bottom. For example, winter and spring fish will penetrate to the highest accessible parts of the river and spawn in the main river and its many tributaries. The summer run occupies the central river system and its tributaries, while the autumn run occupy the lowest part of the river systems and their tributaries. Some grilse will also penetrate to the upper river and its tributaries.

It is often not realised that salmon spawn both in the main river and its tributaries. Even the smallest burn is of the utmost import-ance for spawning purposes provided it has a clean, stable gravel bed. I have on many occasions seen salmon spawning in a hill drain hardly wide enough to accomdate two fish when they are lying side by side. These tiny water courses are often spring fed and seldom dry out.

The stock of a salmon river, provided its water quality is acceptable, is almost entirely controlled firstly by the size of the river and its tributaries, secondly by the number of fish that the river's spawning facilities can accommodate, and thirdly by the number of fry and parr that the river's food supply is capable of supporting. Obviously the larger the river is the more it can produce. In Scotland the river Tay has the largest catchment and this is the only river that accommodates all four runs of fish. The bigger rivers such as the Dee, Spey, Tweed, Ness, Annan and Nith accommodate three runs and most of our other east coast rivers and a few more on the north and west coast facilitate both a spring and a summer run or a summer and autumn run. The smaller east coast rivers such as the Lossie and Bervie and many more west and north-west coast rivers accommodate only one, the summer run.

If a river's spawning grounds become over-crowded this leads to over-cutting of existing salmon redds. This is always to the detriment of the earlier running fish as it is they who spawn first, therefore it is their ova that are destroyed in the process.

Likewise if the number of fry produced in a river system is greater than the food productivity of that river, then numbers are reduced by wastage. This leads to poorer quality smolts being produced and is not desirable. Density levels on the nursery areas of our river systems are of utmost importance and can often become over-saturated by careless re-stocking operations on nursery areas that are already fully stocked.

It must always be remembered that, as far as a salmon river fishery is concerned, early running fish are the most valuable asset that any river can have. The reasons of course for this are that these fish assure an early start to the season and therefore prolong the duration of it, they are available in the river for anglers to exploit longer than any other runs, and their commercial value is a premium.

I believe that all the named runs of salmon regenerate fish with similar characteristics, for example, spring runs regenerate spring fish and so on. Whether this is caused by genetic or environmental reasons or a combination of both is difficult to tell. If I am not correct in this assumption then logically we could expect to find spring runs of salmon in all of our river systems.

The main essential for successful salmon regeneration in a river system is the need for stability; stability not only of water flow but also stability of the bed and banks of the river, particularly the banks above and around the areas of the river system where spawning takes place.

The act of spawning is a highly technical operation and to understand it is best to explain it fully.

The ova requires to be planted six to nine inches deep in good, clean, open gravel so that the ova can breath during the incubation period, which can vary from three to five months. Good spawning gravel is often a scarce commodity in even the longest rivers. Its main requisites are that it must be loose and workable, not compacted, and it must be stable because if a salmon spawns on insecure gravel both that and the ova incubating in it will be washed away before the ova can hatch. The best spawning fords are usually found on a down gradient either at the head or the tail of a gravelly pool or on

Falls Pool – River Cassley.
Impassable until the water temperature rises to 52°F.

a gravelly incline between pools where there is a reasonably fast current. The ideal spawning depth is between nine inches and three feet below the surface with a current speed of around twelve to thirteen inches per second. Water flows of less than three inches per second at the surface are normally unacceptable.

The method used by the female fish to cut her redd is to turn on her side and flap her tail hard down on to the surface of the bed, whipping it back again; this flapping motion creates a type of force and suction which dislodges the gravel from the surface of the bed thereby creating a depression. The reason that the current speed is necessary is because the water flow drifts the debris she has loosened downstream and away from her working. If no flow existed then the gravel would merely fall back into place. Having made the initial depression in the gravel, the hen fish then moves into it and through the use of a rubbing motion with the blade of her tail and ventral fins she eventually deepens the hollow to the necessary spawning depth. Finally she manipulates two large stones into place at the bottom of the depression.

When she is ready to begin the act of spawning she enters the depression and goes into what is called the crouched position with her vent lodged firmly between these two large stones. As soon as the male sees her in this position he immediately draws alongside and the two fish make a simultaneous ejection of milt and ova. The female then moves immediately upstream of the first depression and begins to cut a second one. The gravel dislodged from this covers the fertilised eggs of her first ejection. An average female ejects approximately two thousand eggs into each depression and will require four or more ejections to empty herself. Even after making four depressions for these she still has to cut one more in order to cover her final ejection. The completed result of her work is known as a redd which appears to look like a small mound on the surface of the river bed with a depression immediately upstream.

Nursery, or feeding areas of a river system are, as I have already said, the second most important commodity. It is the productivity of these areas that mainly control the number of smolts that can be produced by the river. Once the yolk sack of the aelvin has been absorbed into the little fish's system, the fry has to forage for itself to obtain the food to sustain itself in future life. At the same time it has to protect itself from the many bird and fish predators that lurk in the waters into which it has just emerged from its gravel nest beneath the river bed. Therefore the two main requirements of a good nursery area are firstly a good, clean water supply of adequate pH value, and secondly an adequate bed and bank cover on the nursery area to afford these little fish a plentiful supply of refuge places where they can hide safely from their predators. The temperature of the water is also of the utmost importance because this controls the amount of dissolved oxygen available in the water. If the water temperature rises to an unacceptable level then the little fish will suffocate.

The lowest pH value acceptable to the salmonid species is 4.6, and I often compare the productivity of nursery areas with that of agricultural land. For example, feeding areas with a pH value of 6.5–7.5 compare favourably with the best arable land. It is in these conditions that high nutrient food, such as fresh water shrimps and snails, thrive as well as most other types of fish fauna. Areas with pH values of 5.5–6.5 can be compared with marginal arable land and these areas can support varying water-borne invertebrates and have an adequate productivity from this type of food supply. The areas with a pH level of 4.6–5.5 can be compared with hill grazing and have a poor productivity of food supply, however terrestial insects blown on to the surface of the water often play a significant part in improving food supplies of this type of nursery area.

The presence of algal growth and other types of weed growth on nursery areas play an important part in helping the productivity, because it is on these that water-borne invertebrates and other types of insects feed and breed, and any nursery area that lacks these is very much the poorer in consequence. Algal growth relies entirely on sunlight to promote it and if this light is shaded from the surface of the water, the productivity of that nursery area is retarded in consequence.

Bank cover serves a double purpose. Vegetation and tree growth on the edge of the river provides a very useful food supply of terrestial insects as well as affording a source of shade during the hottest periods of the year. The overhanging or undermined banks can also provide a safe refuge where little fish can dart underneath to escape from predators. Heavy, dense shading however retards bank cover growth and any use of weed or brush killers close to the bank, quite apart from the danger of pollution, can have disastrous consequences. Apart from the fact that these acts destroy this valuable supplier of insects, shade and cover, the stability of the bank is also jeopardised because the root growth of vegetation binds the edge of the bank securely and is the best fortification a river bank can have in resisting erosion.

Bed cover is another essential requisite to any nursery area whether it be in the form of boulders, stones, gravel or weed growth, because it is beneath these that the little feeding fish can hide when under threat from fish or bird predators, or from the sun. If one approaches a nursery area carefully one can see the little fish spread out, swimming around as they forage for their food but if one makes a careless movement they immediately scurry for cover and in a few seconds none can be seen because they are hidden under crevices of the stones and gravel of the river bed. Similarly, when one is electric shocking a nursery area to obtain a density count of the feeding population, there is absolutely nothing to be seen, yet one only has to probe under rocks, banks, or close to the stones and gravel on the surface of the river bed and countless little fry and parr appear stunned out of these crevices. A plain, sandy-bedded pool affords no shelter for the little fish and it is in situations like this that predators and high water temperatures are able to decimate fry stocks to a mere fraction of their former population due entirely to lack of cover.

Any reduction in water quality affecting the productivity of the insect life in that stream and any reductions in bed and bank cover can have a very serious effect on these nursery areas and consequently the number of smolts that leave these areas when the time for migration comes.

There is absolutely no doubt that the breeding areas of a river system are the lynchpin which control the number of smolts produced by that river. The simple stark fact of salmon management is that unless the breeding and feeding areas are kept in good repair with a healthy, productive capability then strong smolt runs cannot be expected to migrate from these areas to the sea. Any failure of the spawning potential of the river system or any retardation of the productivity of the nursery areas will result in a drastic lowering of the number of smolts produced. Unfortunately in this modern era this fact is completely disregarded and everything from nets and poaching to predators are made the scapegoat for the serious decline in salmon stocks. Therefore it is wise to study whether, in the last twenty years or more, there has been any major change to conditions now reigning on these breeding and feeding areas of our river systems, the very lifeline of our salmon stocks.

LAND AND WATER RESOURCE DEVELOPMENT

During the post war period there has been a substantial change of land use as well as land development which has materially effected the catchment of many of the Scottish river systems. The most significant change of land use has been the planting of hill grazing land for forestry purposes by both the Forestry Commission and private landowners. There has been, at the same time, a real attempt to improve hill grazings by extensive hill drainage schemes, most of which are heavily grant aided by central government. Many hills roads have also been constructed to improve access not only for agriculture and forestry purposes, but also sporting purposes. Finally, large areas of the upper catchment of the river systems have been developed for both water supply and hydro-electric purposes. Many of these improvements to the land surrounding the river system and the development of water resources have in different ways created problems that have affected the productivity of these rivers as producers of salmon stocks. I detail below some of the problems that occur as a result of these improvements.

AGRICULTURE

Hill Drainage: The modern method employed to drain moor and hill land in Scotland is by using a Cuthbertson plough draining along a contour. This is a very effective method of mechanical drainage whereby a drain twelve to fifteen inches deep and approximately twelve inches wide can be cut through peat and moor land, leaving the upturned sod from the furrow along the edge of the drain. Many of these drains zigzag across the hillside and are eventually led directly into a burn, a larger drain, or the main river system.

Provided the sole of the plough does not penetrate the peat crust little erosion occurs and after the initial peat sludge has been washed away, little sediment is discharged. After a long dry period, however, the edges of the drain can crumble with weathering. When the first rains come after a drought a large sediment load can be carried down these drains with the resultant discolouration of the main water course and sludge deposits forming on the river bed.

If the sole of the plough breaks through the peat crust and exposes soil or gravel pan, a thing which often happens on the

149

steeper hillsides, knolls or banks of burns, erosion can occur and this can become serious because of the velocity of water running in the drain which removes the fine silt, sand and gravel which have never been subjected to weathering before. In some cases large deposits of sand, silt and gravel are discharged from these drains into the burn and water courses into which they flow. The actual point of discharge from the drain to the water course is often one of the worst places where bank erosion occurs.

Cases of erosion in some of these drains to a depth of two to three feet in five years is fairly common and there are cases where some of these drains have eroded to a depth greater than eight feet in the same period.

Land Drainage: These drains are normally V-shaped and drain the meadow land between the hill slopes and main water course. When they are first dug, large quantities of silt and sand sludge loosened by the work are washed down into the main water course. Deposits of this sludge will continue to be washed down these drains during times of flood until the bottom and sides of the drains stabilise. These drains normally have a very low fall and over the years can become silted up and choked with weed growth. When these drains are coupled to the smaller hill drains this silting up can often be aggravated by deposits carried into them from the smaller drains. This means that these drains have to be frequently cleaned out with the resultant influx of sludge into the water ways. On the other hand they can, be a useful producer of invertebrates on which young fish feed.

In some cases burns, or even sections of main tributaries are canalised for drainage purposes. Not only does this destroy the stability of these watercourses, but also it often leads to an increase of water velocity over these sections. Both these alterations to the natural regime of the watercourse cause an influx of loose gravel, sand and silt to be released downstream of these operations during spate flows for a considerable time into the future.

Hill Roads: Poorly constructed roads, often with inadequate culverts and drainage ditches, are bulldozed into the open hill to serve agricultural improvements to the hill. When these are first made a large extent of gravel, sand and silt is exposed to weather for the first time, and this often leads to considerable erosion of the banks of the road, and the surface of the road at times of heavy rainfall, can become a water course. This causes large quantities of sand, silt and gravel to be washed into the neighbouring burns. Hill roads made to serve sporting purposes have largely the same effect.

Sheep and Stock: Particularly during hot weather in summer sheep can cause erosion of drains, banks of roads and burns by rubbing up against these. Indiscriminate burning of heath land can often aggravate this situation.

FORESTRY

Ploughing for Planting: The modern method of planting trees requires the ground to be ploughed prior to planting. Normally the ground is ploughed with six to seven feet between the furrows and a forty-five degree cross furrow drain cut at fairly frequent intervals to catch the water from the furrows and prevent scouring. On the steeper slopes it is sometimes not possible to put in this forty-five degree drain and on these slopes each furrow becomes a potential water course. Very often on this type of ground there is only a very shallow peat crust, and in many cases gravel, soil and sand are exposed to weather conditions they have not been subjected to before and are, therefore, prone to erosion. On the flow ground and more peaty areas of the hill after the initial influx of peat sludge from these furrows little erosion occurs, and with the absence of stock there is little to start fresh erosion of these furrows. Once the trees have reached over eight years of age their roots begin to bind the exposed surfaces and further erosion is unlikely.

Forestry Drainage: The cross furrow is normally led into a main leader, small burn or other natural water course. Those draining peaty land in the initial stages will run off deposits of peat sludge and silt, which can badly discolour the main water course and cause large deposits to form on the bed of the water courses.

Those draining the harder hilly areas and lower slopes can carry substantial quantities of silt, sand and gravel into the main water courses for a considerable time after they have been made.

Roads: Forestry roads after they are first put in can suffer a certain amount of erosion in the initial stages, but are normally of higher quality than other hill roads and soon stabilise. Because of the absence of stock in the forests this erosion is not usually aggravated. Tree roots and other vegetation soon bind the banks.

Trees: The planting of conifers has seriously affected the productivity of some Scottish streams, leading to a paucity of invertebrate and fish fauna in streams flowing through mature forest, with a dense tree canopy preventing sunlight encouraging algal growth and ground vegetation. This effect can have direct repercussions on the value of nursery areas.

Flow regime in afforested areas is further accentuated by water loss from the tree canopy interception of precipitation, and transpiration. Work in the Institute of Hydrology on Plynlimon in mid-Wales has shown quite conclusively that the trees intercept substantially more water than open moorland, and this has adverse effects in long dry periods and periods of irregular rainfall. It was shown that out of a total rainfall of 2700 mm, 780 mm were lost as interception and 310 mm as transpiration, producing a total water loss of more than twice the potential open water evaporation. It is unlikely that the nursery streams can afford the water losses that these afforested areas incur.

There is evidence that in afforested areas, due to the leaching out of nutrients from the soil and the deposit of pine needles from the trees, the pH value of the waterways draining the areas can in some cases be lowered appreciably. This is especially true of spruce forests where it has been known for pH values of 7 to be lowered to 3.2. This can be extremely serious as the pH value of 4.6 is the lowest value acceptable to young salmonids.

Spraying: It is necessary at times for forest owners to spray in order to control certain insects that cause damage to trees. This is normally carried out by aerial spraying. As many nursery areas of the salmon and trout stocks of the country lie within forestry areas great care must be taken to ensure the fact that the sprays used are not toxic to these small fish or to the food and insect life on which they depend for their survival.

The chief effect of all roadmaking and drainage activities is that all the eroded material is carried down the minor tributaries into either major tributaries or the main river. In cases where these improvements are carried out on the head waters of the river or tributary systems they can have a serious effect on the spawning and feeding areas of the river. The worst results are as follows:

Water Flow: When man-made drains cover a wide part of the catchment area of a burn, tributary or river the regime of the water course turns from seepage drainage to quick run off. This makes the regime of the river far more flashy, rising quickly and falling equally quickly, high water conditions last only a few days instead of a much longer period when seepage drainage prevailed. This reduces the number of days when the fishing is at its best.

This quick run off of the water no longer allows the same amount of water to seep into the sub-strata. This in turn can lead to failure of spring supply and in some cases can result in lower minimum dry weather flow in these water courses and longer periods of dry weather flow. Spring water supplies have a constant water temperature of 42°F at source. These supplies act as a cooling agent in the summer months and a heating agent during the winter.

A flashy river regime normally aggravates erosion of banks and burns, tributaries and rivers causing dirtier floods and resultant movement of sand, silt and gravel in the water courses.

Redds: A large movement of silt, sand and gravel in the river system can make spawning redds unstable. Silt and sand can compact the spawning gravel thereby making it unworkable. It can also prevent the percolation of water through the redd, thereby smothering any ova which are incubating in the redd at that time.

Large deposits of gravel moving through a river systems can either be deposited on top of existing redds thereby smothering them or if the fish spawn on these freshly deposited gravel banks, the eggs and the gravel are liable to be washed away in the next spate because of the instability of the gravel.

Salmon Pools: These can be seriously affected by a large movement of silt, sand and gravel and in many cases the angling and holding capabilities of these pools can be completely ruined if large deposits of gravel are washed into them. Even if the gravel banks form on the edge of pools they can alter the current flow through the pools and add to the risk of further bank erosion.

Pools with rock ledges or large stones in the bottom of them are particularly liable to hold gravel moving down the river bed and once it is lodged between these ledges or behind big stones it is extremely difficult to remove.

Feeding Areas: Any reduction in pH value of the water course reduces the amount of feed available for young salmon on the nursery areas of the water course. Likewise, any retarding of algal growth on feeding areas creates a similar problem. In both cases this leads to a reduction of productivity of these areas.

Erosion of Banks: Once banks of burns, tributaries or rivers begin to erode it is extremely difficult to stop this erosion without great expense. Continual movement of silt, sand and gravel down the bed of the burn can completely ruin the stability of the burn particularly the smaller burns. This reduces the feeding capacity of that stream and it is often these waters which are of the greatest importance as nursery feeding grounds.

Some of these smaller burns can become so overloaded with silt and sludge that they are completely incapable of cleansing themselves. Good spawning and feeding areas can have their gravel beds completely submerged by this silt and they can then no longer be used for spawning.

Water Loss: After a long dry summer, water courses running through afforested areas are often drawn down so low that on occasions adult fish wishing to enter these at spawning time are unable to do so. They are forced, therefore, to spawn elsewhere, probably on already populated areas.

Gravel Extraction: It is common practice for landowners or tenants to remove gravel from the beds of burns or rivers for road making purposes. This not only causes instability of that section where the gravel has been removed but also if this act is carried out during spawning time or when the ova is incubating in the gravel, considerable damage can be caused to salmon stocks in that area.

Fish Farms and Hatcheries: Afforestation and land drainage on the catchment areas of burns being used as a water supply for fish farms and hatcheries can create grave problems if the silt and sediment load carried by these burns is increased in any way or if the pH value or water quality is altered. In the same way this applies to burns, which have the right potential required for fish farm or hatchery use, but have so far not been exploited.

DEVELOPMENT OF WATER RESOURCES

In the 1950s especially, vast areas of good spawning ground and nursery areas were drowned out when reservoirs were created for either water supply or hydro-electric purposes, and many of these were sited on the most important spawning areas on the upper catchment of the rivers. At the same time access to feeding grounds above the impounded area was in some cases impeded by badly designed fish passes, or else completely de-barred in cases where no fish passes were installed on the dam. A further problem caused to migratory fish stocks by these impoundment works was that the brown trout population in these reservoirs benefitted greatly from the increased food supply of the newly flooded area, and therefore not only multiplied in numbers but also grew appreciably in size in consequence. This meant that these trout not only competed with migratory fish stocks, both in the limited spawning and feeding grounds that remained available above the dammed area, but also in many cases preyed on the feeding fry and parr on the nursery area itself, as well as on the smolts as they migrated through the reservoir area in the early summer.

What people fail to realise is that the result of either a total loss of spawning and feeding areas or a partial reduction in the productivity of these, creates not one but two problems. Firstly, those that are flooded out are destroyed for ever, causing an immediate percentage reduction in the overall production of that particular river system. Secondly, when the native stock of these lost areas return to spawn, they are no longer able to use the flooded areas and therefore fall back or push forward on to the already fully populated spawning areas so that they can spawn themselves. The immediate result of this phenomenon is over-crowding of the spawning and feeding grounds, which is always to the detriment of the early running fish who spawn first.

When river systems were developed for hydro-electricity, it was often necessary to augment the water resources of that river by diverting water from neighbouring catchments through into the catchment that was being developed. In most cases this was achieved by tunnelling through the hillside and allowing the water to flow from these neighbouring catchments by gravity into the impounded area. In some cases this affected certain tributaries of the neighbouring river and in other cases the main river itself was diverted. Rivers that were robbed of their headwaters by these means were naturally seriously damaged because of the drastic reduction in their river flow regime. In many cases important feeding and spawning areas upstream of the diversion dam were de-barred for all time to the salmon species. A glaring example of this type of work is the Perthshire river, Garry, running adjacent to the main A9 between Blair Atholl and Dalwhinnie, which is so badly affected that during dry weather periods all that is left of this very important spawning tributary of the Tay system is a dry, rock-strewn river bed. Other examples are the headwaters of the river Carron in Easter Ross, which is diverted into the Conon hydro-electric scheme and the headwaters of the rivers Cassley, Brora and Vagisty (a tributary of the Naver), all of which are diverted into the Shin hydro-scheme.

The flow regime of the river where the main dam is sited is also badly affected because the section of the river below the dam is subjected to compensation flows for much of the year. This in turn can drastically alter fish movement and behaviour in these sections of the river, as well as affecting the spawning and feeding areas downstream of the dam. Sometimes access to spawning areas above the dam is either impeded or de-barred as a result of badly designed fish passes on the dam.

In some cases the generated water, after passing through the turbine, is discharged down the main river course and this naturally causes the flow in these rivers to fluctuate drastically throughout the year, creating problems to both spawning and feeding stocks. In other cases the water from the main dam is led by a tunnel, adjacent to the river system, to a generating station some distance below the dam, and then returned to the main river course a short distance from the mouth. In these cases the section of the river between the dam and where the water is returned to the river course is subjected to compensation flow regimes for the entire year. These sections of the river only get flood flows when and if the dam overflows. This materially affects the angling potential as well as the productivity of the spawning areas that remain viable. Examples of rivers where the water is generated on the dam are the Beauly and Conon, whilst the Shin is an example of the latter. Water quality and temperatures of both rivers that have had their headwaters diverted and also the rivers actually developed for generating purposes can be materially affected by these schemes, normally to the detriment of the fish stocks in the rivers.

Not all rivers are affected by the varying land development and water resource development activities. Some rivers are very badly affected by these schemes, others have an appreciable amount of the catchment of a particular tributary affected, whilst a very few have escaped completely unblemished.

These problems I have listed above can have very serious effects on the salmon stocks. When fish kills occur either as a result of poison, poaching or pollution incidents, fishery owners can quantify the loss by the number of fish killed and can, if necessary, take remedial steps by re-stocking with fry and parr the following year if it is thought necessary. However, in cases of damage caused by development works, in most cases fishery owners are oblivious to the damage to stocks or are in no position to quantify the damage that has been done until such a time as a marked stock decline in the river system or part of the river system occurs. Even then the real reason for this failure is often overlooked.

Many people are also very loathe to admit that over-crowding of certain sections of the river system can seriously damage spring runs of fish or salmon stocks in the river system. However, it is very interesting to note that famous spring rivers such as the Beauly, Conon and Shin completely lost their spring runs as soon as they were involved in the development for hydro power and one would have to think hard to find a river that was developed for hydro power whose spring run has not been drastically affected. The reason for this is the loss of spawning and feeding grounds used by the spring run which in turn leads to an over-crowding and over-cutting of the redds on the available spawning areas.

There is absolutely no doubt that these activities must take a great deal of the blame for the overall decline of salmon stocks in Scotland. There is also no doubt that there will be more land and water resources development in the future, so it would be wise, therefore, to recognise the problems and try to devise some means of overcoming them in the future, as in some cases the damage could well escalate. For example, thirty years ago the forestry managers were averse to planting trees in ground over a certain altitude, and in many cases salmon stocks could use spawning grounds above this level and were often, therefore, unaffected by these works. Now, however, with improved forestry techniques it is possible to plant trees successfully on higher ground and the planting line has now been extended to approximately the same altitude as salmon stocks are able to spawn at.

For many years it has been necessary for forestry and agricultural bodies to discuss which land should be planted for trees and which ground should be left for agricultural purposes, but never has it been necessary to consult District Fishery Boards concerning these aspects. Surely it is time that all main rural industries should liase more with each other in order to prevent the development of one industry destroying the asset of another. I strongly believe that more consultation should take place prior to large development schemes between forestry, agriculture, fishery, and purifications boards, and owners, in order to try and reduce or overcome this type of problem.

PREDATORS

Predators are another factor which can have a material effect on salmon stock, both in fresh water and during their sea-feeding life. The worst fish predators in fresh water that prey on feeding fry and parr are either trout, eels, perch or pike, whilst the worst bird predators are the diving species such as mergansers, cormorants and goosanders.

Pike are present in many of our river systems in Scotland with the exception of some of the smaller west coast rivers and those in the north and west of Scotland. It is said that pike were mainly introduced to Scotland by monks, as this was a cheap, useful source of food greatly favoured by them. It is certainly true to say that wherever there was a monastery pike stocks in the area are fairly abundant! The Conon river system in Ross-shire is the furthest north that pike are to be found. There is no doubt that these fish do take a considerable toll of smolt migrations as they descend through the loch system and also they prey on fry, parr and smolts in the river systems.

Brown, rainbow and sea trout can also take a considerable toll of fry and parr on their nursery areas and all these fish, and their offspring, compete with the young salmon for the limited food supply available in fresh water. Since the last war there has been a vast increase in the number of anglers throughout the country, as a result it has become common practice to re-stock rivers with large quantities of both brown and rainbow trout. In many cases this has resulted in the trout gaining predominance over the salmon on many of our feeding and spawning grounds, much to the detriment of the salmon.

Mergansers, goosanders and cormorants have always been a serious menace to salmon stocks especially during the smolt migration where they take a heavy toll. Smolts are easy prey for these birds, who can swim underwater for long distances. They can eat upwards of five smolts per day and on more than one occasion I have found up to nine smolts in a merganser and thirteen in the other species. Considering that we expect a 10% return from smolts, this virtually means one adult salmon per pair of adult birds a day. Or looking at it from another way, smolts fetch 120p each at the present time, so surely this is a cost and wastage that the industry can ill afford. Since the Wildlife and Countryside Act 1982 these birds can now only be shot under licence in Scotland. In 1986 the Nature Conservancy Council, who advises the Department of Agriculture and Fisheries (Scotland) on the issue of licences, have decided to curtail the duration of these licences to a four month period, covering the smolt run. It would seem from the Fishery Manager's point of view that everything must be protected in this modern era except salmon stocks!

During their sea life the dangerous predator on salmon is the seal, both the Atlantic Grey and the Common seal. In 1914 Hesketh was responsible for bringing in the Grey Seal Conservation Act because at that time it was estimated that there were only 1500 seals around the shores of the United Kingdom. Since then we have seen the grey seal population escalate by some 5% a year, leading to a population of around 15,000 in the 1940s, 30,000 in the 1960s and 88,000 in 1985. In 1985 we were told by the Secretary of State for Scotland, after extreme pressure from Greenpeace and other conservation bodies, that all seal culls in Scotland were to be suspended until further notice. This, in effect, will mean that by 1990 there will be over 100,000 seals and by the turn of the century, 150,000 around our shores a substantial proportion of the world's population of the grey seal. As these mammals eat approximately fifteen pounds of white fish or salmon a day each, the cost to the white fish and salmon industry in this country is at the moment astronomical and this, too, will escalate.

If true a simple calculation shows that this amounts to 481,800,000lb of fish per annum. Even allowing the fact that 25% of their diet consists of non-commercial fish and also deducting an allowance for the time that the cow seals are breeding, it is reasonable to assume that the white fish and salmon industry are losing over 300 million pounds of fish per annum to the grey seals alone. When no fish can be purchased for under £1 per pound today, it is immaterial whether one calculates the loss to the industry in pounds weight or £s sterling, it is still 300,000,000 per annum.

I think it is questionable when half the world is starving for want of food that the British Government, when negotiating with the EEC and other countries for white fish and salmon quotas, in effect demands one quota to sell and eat and another quota to feed a menagerie. We are told by the SMRU research unit in their recent report on seals that these mammals have a diet that consists largely of sand eels. Did nature really give the grey seal a jaw structure such as it has with large teeth, to drink fish soup?

The grey seal is particularly damaging to the spring run of salmon. These mammals move inshore during the winter to prey on cod and other sea fish that are close to the shore at that time of year, and when these fish move further out to sea in the spring, these seals are ideally placed to intercept the spring fish homing into their rivers of origin. When the spring runs were strong in the 1960s it mattered little if a run of fish, numbering about one hundred, had to run the gauntlet of five seals in an estuary but at the present time when a run of ten salmon have to run the gauntlet of twenty seals in the same situation, it is a very different story.

Naturally, when the water flow in our own rivers is low salmon are held back at the mouth of the river, waiting to enter the river system, and here seals can wreak havoc on these fish congregated in such an enclosed area and can seriously decimate both the grilse and salmon runs throughout the year, under these conditions.

Common seals normally found inside the larger estuaries or on islands round the coast can often take their toll on salmon, grilse and sea trout, but being much smaller than the grey seal do not decimate stocks to the same extent.

If only the public realised that the pretty little seal cub that looks so angelic when born, grows into a blood-thirsty killer, weighing ten hundredweight and more, they might think twice before joining the conservation lobby.

The problem with seal, like all predators, is that they often kill for want of killing and not just for what they need to eat. A rogue seal can easily destroy half a dozen fish and devour only one or two. The seal mainly catches fish by impaling it on the claws of its flipper and many fish escape badly wounded. Very often as the seal strikes the nail will come into contact with the armoured scales from the salmon's back downwards, and will leave a semi-circular scoured line down the fish's side before penetrating its soft under-belly, this part of the fish often breaks and the fish escapes with a very nasty wound. These wounded fish are often caught by anglers but those which do not fall prey to the fisherman become a disease risk after a period of time in fresh water.

This semi-circular scour line down the fish's side is very often mistaken by anglers as a net mark, especially if there is no penetration to the under-belly, as the area where the claw mark comes in contact with the fish is nearly always de-scaled.

Having captured its prey, the seal wrenches the skin from its fully alive, wriggling victim before devouring the flesh and leaving the backbone, head and fins, with the skin still attached, as debris on the shore. Scientists over many years have proved catagorically that seal prey on salmon by examining the actual contents of the seal's stomach. This showed that seals foraging close to the mouth of a salmon river or coastline contained 15% of the remains of salmon in their stomachs, whilst those foraging further offshore contained only 5%. The latest research into seal damage by the SMRU decided to use the faeces of seals to obtain evidence of their diet, and this evidence was based on the number of oeseriths found in the faeces. This tiny bone is found in the ear of fish and is not dissolved in the digestion process. Not surprisingly they found numerous oeseriths from sand eels and small fish in the faeces and have concluded, because of this evidence, that seals depend largely on these types of fish as the main part of their diet. The white fish and salmon industries are highly suspicious of this type of evidence because firstly it is a well known fact that seals discard the heads of the bigger types of fish on which they prey and also the bony parts of the fins, so therefore the oeserith of these fish and other hard parts which are unlikely to be dissolved are naturally absent in the faeces. Secondly, as sand eels and small fish are a staple diet of cod, salmon, sea trout and other large fish, the oeserith present in the stomachs of these fish when they fall victim to seals will be, in turn, devoured by the seal and therefore bound to be found in the faeces.

It is high time people stopped dragging their feet over this most serious problem, because it will not go away but only get worse. It is, therefore, necessary to face up to the problem and not sweep it under the carpet like it has been by many successive governments. No-one wishes to make the species extinct, but the population of the seals must be reduced to reasonable proportions.

Other predators at sea are some species of sea fish, who prey on the salmon during its varied life stages at sea, as well as cormorants, diving birds and gulls. Thes fish and birds also take smaller sized sea trout who feed around the coasts and estuaries as well as taking their toll on smolts shortly after they have entered the sea.

NETS

We now turn to probably the most controversial subject of all, namely nets. For centuries, salmon stocks have been exploited by legal and illegal netsmen in the sea, around the coast, in the estuaries, and in the olden days it was common practice to exploit salmon stocks some distance up the river by nets. This part of the chapter will relate to legal nets and I shall deal with illegal nets when I discuss the poaching problem.

When salmon rights were given by Crown Grant to private individuals as a hereditable right, regardless of where the fishery was sited, these included the full right to exploit fish by both rod and line and net. This meant that all owners of angling rights anywhere on the river system could exercise their netting rights if they so wished, as well as exercising their rod and line rights.

In 1862 and 1868 Salmon Fishery (Scotland) Acts curtailed the use of fixed engines, such as bag and fly nets, to areas of the coast-line outside the estuary limits. Only sweep netting by net and coble was permitted inside estuary limits and up river, with the one exception, that individuals who had the right of cruise fishing, a separate right, were allowed to continue to exercise this right.

During the last century nearly all netting stations up-river, above the tidal limits, have been phased out, either as a result of being bought out by river improvement association or private individuals and only in isolated cases, on very few rivers, is up-river sweep and coble netting exercised at the present time.

It has always been the accepted practice that the breeding nation should be allowed the greatest cull of salmon stocks produced. Nets are an essential and integral part of fish management for the simple reason that they are the only means of reducing large salmon runs to proportions which the river of origin is capable of supporting for regeneration purposes. If it was left to rod and line fisheries to cull these runs of salmon they would be quite incapable of doing so, and the end result would be over-crowding of both feeding and spawning areas. This would have a detrimental effect on the early running fish and eventually on the entire salmon stocks of the river. Over-crowding produces the risk of disease, particularly of the type known as furrunculosis which can, if it breaks out, wipe out large numbers of salmon in a matter of days. Any person who has witnessed an outbreak of this type of disease will never forget such an incident, because even the smell of the rotting carcasses would deter one from going within several hundred yards of the river. These outbreaks normally occur at an optimum water temperature, around 65°F.

As well as the breeding nation, it is perfectly right and proper that the nation around whose shores these salmon feed, should be allowed a quota cull as a grazing right, because if our salmon did not feed on the lush food supply around those nation's shores some other fish would, and these fish could be exploited on a commercial basis. This cull, however, should be closely related to the productivity of the breeding nation at that time, instead of a figure being pulled out of the sky with complete disregard of the stock situation in the breeding country. If more heed had been taken of this vital necessity when the Greenland fishery first came into being in the 1960s, the ramification of this fishery would not have been so pronnounced, and the damage to earlier running fish stocks might have been far less than it is at the moment.

What, however, no fishery manager in the world can condone is the interceptory fishery that exploits fish stocks on their homeward migration between the feeding grounds at sea and their rivers of origin. Any nation that exercises a fishery of this nature is allowing a pirate fishery. They are exploiting fish stocks purely for greed and gain towards which they have not paid one single penny piece as far as breeding and feeding of that catch goes. As a British subject it is galling to have to admit that the most glaring example of this type of interceptory fishery is the one carried out by the Northumberland and Yorkshire Water Authority, off the north-east coast of England. This fishery, is intercepting approximately 90% of its catch from salmon stocks destined for rivers in Scotland. The Scottish component in the catch of this fishery is so significant that it adds up to approximately 60% of the total annual salmon catch of the whole of England and Wales. Without this Scottish element England and Wales could no longer be regarded as a significant Atlantic salmon producer.

In a recent DAFS consultation document on salmon fisheries it is freely admitted that drift net fisheries for salmon are harmful to salmon stocks and it advises that drift netting for salmon should be banned around the English and Welsh coastline, with the exception of the Northumberland/Yorkshire area.

Why this area should be exempted from the ban is difficult to understand. Not only does this fishery drastically reduce the number of salmon returning to their rivers of origin, from the Tweed north to the Esks, and thereby reduces employment in salmon fisheries in these areas, but it also prevents and impedes scientific research experiments from being carried out with any degree of accuracy on these rivers. It further prevents salmon ranching enterprises, which have been successfully carried out in the norther hemisphere, from being undertaken on the east coast of Scotland. Ranching cannot be a viable commercial concern when large numbers of the reared fish are being intercepted, literally on the last lap of their homeward migration. This fishery also creates severe problems when the United Kingdom Government is negotiating with other countries of the North Atlantic Convention over the salmon quota and policy. Time and time again we in the industry are told by the Greenlanders and other counterparts to put our own house in order first before expecting them to be sympathetic to our problem.

Many anglers advocate drastic curbing of the legal netting operations around the Scottish coastline. They demand longer weekend slack periods, much longer annual close seasons and at the same time a ban of all netting during low river flows. All these things sound very easy to achieve but the implication of carrying out these stringent regulations could be counter-productive. The legal, financial and administration difficulties that would arise as a result are amongst the many reasons why these suggestions should be rejected.

First of all, the very presence of the legal netsmen offer the river system a high degree of protection against poaching in sensitive areas such as enclosed estuaries and coastal bays and harbour areas, as they ply their trade. This presence deters poachers from setting hang nets and working sweep and drift nets where they could wreak havoc to salmon runs if they remained undetected, and if these nets are successfully set they are able to detect and remove them.

The very fact that this side of the industry is well equipped with boats give an added flexibility to the bailiff staff of the Fishery Board at absolutely no cost, whereas if these legal tacksmen were

164

not present the cost of equipping the bailiffs with the necessary boats to deal with the poachers in these areas would be exorbitant.

In recent years many of these netsmen have been put out of business because of the drastic decline in net catches, and in consequence many Boards have not only lost this priceless form of protection but also a very large part of their revenue which accrued from these netting operations in the form of assessment.

One of the mainstay's of the success of the 1862/68 legislation was the dual source of revenue to the Board from both strong net and rod fisheries. In many cases the former provided the greater proportion of this finance. Without this share and the built-in protection, (which was afforded without cost), no Board could be in the financial position to maintain the standard of protection required to enable them to carry out their remit, solely on revenue raised by rod fisheries in their district. As I have shown many west coast Boards have found this out to their cost and have lapsed in consequence.

Another mainstay of Scottish legislation has been the fact that both rod and net fisheries are owned by individuals as a separate hereditable right. This has made these individuals far more conscious of the need to conserve salmon stocks in their district in order that they have a valid asset to pass on down to their successors. It is, therefore, in no-one's interest to ruin their fishery by over-netting and be left with a worthless property at the end of the day. That is the reason why net fishery owners on many occasions since their fisheries were de-rated for local authority rates in 1954, have heavily subsidised Fishery Boards to enable them to conserve fisheries in their districts, and have also been in the forefront of promoting and supporting and even financing research in this field.

POACHING

Long gone, unfortunately, are the days when this enterprising occupation was carried out purely to subsidise the stew pot in order to support the family. Now it is mainly a highly sophisticated, organised form of commercial enterprise, often leading to wanton destruction, which in some cases goes as far as to threaten the conservation of salmon stocks in some of our river systems.

There is little doubt that the high value of the commodity in question, the ease of transport and improved refrigeration methods, have all been factors that have helped poachers to thrive, and thus present the threat to salmon stocks they do at the present time.

The fact that central government in Scotland has, during the last thirty years, failed to realise this threat and therefore dragged their feet regarding updating Salmon Fisheries Legislation to combat this menace, has played a very significant part in increasing the pressures placed on salmon stocks from this source.

In the early 1960s the government of that era was alerted by the industry that current legislation pertaining to salmon fisheries was inadequate to deal with the problems of that day. Therefore a committee, under the chairmanship of Lord Hunter, was set up by the government to review the entire position concerning the Salmon and Fresh Water Fisheries in Scotland.

In spite of the fact that this committee submitted their report in 1962, highlighting the fact that there were many inadequacies, none of the successive governments since that time have seen fit to implement any part of the recommendations contained in the report, or any other legislation on the matter, up to 1985.

There is, however, in 1986 at long last a Bill passing through Parliament.

There is no doubt that during the last war poaching activities increased, mainly because many keepers and water bailiffs were called up for active service and few people were available to replace them. The standard of protection on the rivers declined accordingly. However, due to petrol rationing transportation was much inhibited, and this curtailed poaching to one for the pot or small scale commercial work to local food hostels in the vicinity, mainly by gaff, sniggling or net.

It was not till immediately after the war that the deadly poison poaching method first began to rear its ugly head. This invidious method wrought havoc on the stocks of fish in many rivers and often left wanton destruction in its wake, as few poachers knew the power of this ingredient and far too large a charge was used. This resulted in far more fish being killed than the poachers were capable of handling, and after an incident many fish were left dead, strewn around the banks or at the bottom of the pools. Even worse, not only were mature fish the victims, but also many feeding fry, parr and other fresh water fish, as well as fish fauna in the section of the river where the incident took place.

Since the early poison poaching days, professionals in the game have learnt by experience how large a charge to use according to the size of pool being attacked, and generally kill approximately the number of fish they can handle. However, these raids still do untold damage to fry, parr and fish fauna in these pools. Any large numbers of dead fish left after a raid generally points to the fact that either amateurs were involved or the gang was disturbed in the middle of their work.

In 1951 legislation was passed through parliament to close loopholes in the 1862/68 Acts, in order to deal with this new form of poaching. This Act also stiffened penalties considerably for all forms of salmon poaching, fines were increased, jail sentences introduced, and it also allowed for confiscation of gear and transportation in the case of those who were convicted. Unfortunately in many cases those convicted have been dealt with leniently, and this has helped to encourage many renowned poachers to continue their trail of wanton destruction as well as encouraging others to jump on the band wagon.

Wet suits, CB radio, more cars, better roads, monofilament and other types of synthetic, man-made fibre nets have all led to the success of more sophisticated types of gang poaching, well planned, excellently co-ordinated and speedily executed. All of which has made this a very lucrative practice, very difficult to deal with in spite of the increased bailiff and police co-operation, aided by more modern equipment.

After the outbreak of UDN fish disease in salmon stocks in Scotland in 1967, poachers were slightly deterred from carrying out large raids on the river systems because many of the fish caught were marked and affected by the disease and therefore difficult to market. The poaching fraternity soon turned their attention away from actual rivers and concentrated more effort on the estuary and coastal areas, where their prize was of better quality fish. This in turn stretched bailiff resources even further because previously this area of the district was considered to be reasonably safe, and apart from the bailiffs having to check that the legal netsmen were obeying weekend slap close times and close season regulations little time had to be spent in this area. Few Boards, therefore, were in the position to deal quickly with this new threat to the salmon stocks while they were still in the sea. The bailiffs were not equipped with boats and other necessary equipment to tackle this problem, nor did they have sufficient staff. Luckily DAFS soon realised the implication of this menace to salmon stocks and gave great assistance to Boards by diverting resources to help protect salmon stocks around the Scottish coast. Even helicopter patrols were flown on a regular basis to support the surface patrol ships and smaller craft, with great success.

However, land set hang-nets and floating drift nets are extremely difficult to detect and even if found and lifted can easily be replaced at little cost to the operator. This type of net can take a serious toll of salmon following land fall, as they home in to their rivers of origin, as well as providing a very lucrative source of revenue with very much less risk to the operator of being caught. Even if he is charged and convicted the penalties are not so severe as that for poison poaching, where the risk of being caught is greater.

Drift net fishing for salmon in Scotland has been banned since 1962, but in my opinion the legal drift net fishery off the north-east coast of England has encouraged the Scottish white fish fishermen to carry out drift net fishing in Scottish waters even though it is illegal to do so.

Although the Fishery Protection service has curbed this activity to a certain degree, the Scottish coastline is so extensive that it is impossible to stamp out this type of poaching completely.

There is absolutely no doubt that until England and Wales come into line and ban drift net fishing for salmon, like Scotland, no real breakthrough can be expected in stamping out this wasteful form of illegal exploitation of salmon stocks, mainly because these illegal catches can so easily be marketed through legal outlets or else these enable poached fish to be passed through undetected.

Drift or hang net caught fish are often of poor quality because the flesh is bruised, and in many cases the fish are either descaled or wounded. Therefore these fish fetch a poor premium compared with trapped or sweep net caught fish. Many fish that escape from drift nets are wounded and these fish then become a disease risk when they enter their river. Many other fish die in these nets and fall out of them to become crab meat on the sea bed which is a complete waste of a valuable resource. There is therefore little to commend this type of fishery.

Net poaching on the rivers has also been greatly simplified by the new synthetic material that the modern nets are made of. Nets are so light now and of such little bulk that it is quite possible for a person to conceal a useful length of netting on his person without it being conspicuous, and very large lengths of netting can easily be carried in a vehicle. Often poachers use wet suits to help them set the net or even sweep the net through the pool. Those with intimate knowledge of the rivers they are raiding can, with modern equipment, obtain worthwhile catches, regardless of the water height in the river. These gangs are often dropped off early in the evening and collected later by accomplices, with or without their catch, as on some occasions the catch is left hidden in bushes until it is collected sometime after. Often one or more rivers are raided by the same gang on the same night, one vehicle being used to drop and collect the men and an entirely different vehicle used to collect their catch, even up to twenty-four hours later.

Other poachers still prefer to either sniggle fish with large treble hooks and heavy nylon, or else use a gaff or a clique. The latter methods are used mainly at weirs, caulds or waterfalls and quite large hauls of fish can be obtained by any of these methods.

On the coastline, and particularly in estuaries, hang-nets are greatly favoured and these are often set across the bay or off a promontory, anchored to the shore at one end and in the water at the other. Because salmon favour following the coastline, even short lengths of this type of net can provide worthwhile catches. Once again modern synthetic netting and small, torpedo-shaped floats have made hang-net poaching a very deadly, lucrative method. These nets can very easily be set surreptitiously, and are very difficult to detect, by far the most hazardous part of the operation is the removal of the catch from the scene! Again this is often simplified by the network of roads that follow the coast or river and the accomplice can easily disguise himself as an innocent picnicker, enjoying the scenery whilst he waits for the poacher to return with the catch.

LEGISLATION

Many people think the only thing necessary to combat poaching is further legislation on Salmon Fisheries. Although this is important, it is by no means the only problem that has to be dealt with in conserving salmon stocks.

The 1862/68 legislation is one hundred years out of date and although it held Scottish Salmon Fisheries in good stead for very many years, it has now become incapable of dealing with new types of land development, fish farming activities, hydro-electric schemes and many other aspects of salmon fisheries.

In the 1880s the most common use of water resources was to create power for mills. Water was diverted from the main river by means of a weir or cauld and then conducted by a laide downstream to serve the waterwheel. Provisions in the 1868 Act to deal with fish passes and screening of the laides to prevent damage to fish was laid down in schedule G of this Act. It was the kelts and the adult fish entering the laide which were the problem in those days, as smolts on their downward migration came to little harm even if they had to negotiate the mill race and waterwheel itself. Today problems that had never been heard of in the 1880s have to be overcome. Although the Hydro-Electric Development (Scotland) Act 1943 dealt with fishery problems, private hydro schemes are a different matter and are only covered by schedule G of the present legislation. This is completely inadequate as it does not require smolt screening on private hydro intakes or on mill laides which are often used for this purpose, or for fish farm purposes. Large numbers of smolts can therefore be lost due to this deficiency.

Irrigation which is now being used more and more for horticulture and agriculture is not covered under old fishery legislation, in spite of the fact that good feeding tributaries can be virtually dried out by these practices with resulting damage to fish stocks.

In many cases the old legislation has proved itself to be far too rigid and inflexible. For instance it demanded that all rivers in a district must have the same open and close season. There is no doubt this is a retrograde step as each river should be judged on its own merit, and more flexibility is required on this point.

Although the Scottish District Fishery Board is charged with the remit of maintaining, protecting and improving salmon stocks in its district, there is no provision in the legislation whereby district boards even need to be consulted concerning many land developments and other changes of land use which could materially affect the breeding and feeding of salmon stocks. Naturally until district Boards are given some rights for consultation over these matters, conservation of salmon stocks will be in jeopardy.

Even the right to deal with predators has, since the 1880s, been either completely withdrawn or severely curtailed due to the Grey Seal Conservation Act of 1914, Bird Protection Acts or the Wildlife and Countryside Act 1981. All these Acts are designed to conserve some species of mammal or bird but they make the job of the district Board, a statutory body charged with the duty of conserving salmon that much more difficult as well as much more costly.

Boards are entirely financed by their own industry with no public money being made available from central government or regional authorities whatsoever, because salmon fishing is supposed to be a rich man's sport! This line of argument totally fails to realise that salmon fishing is a rural industry. To start with the rod fisheries are open to the public for a very large part of the fishing season. The fact that people come to fish helps to promote tourism, creates employment and provides a spin-off to the rural community and public at large. Yet, unlike other rural industries such as forestry and agriculture, no public funds are available to subsidise or augment the fishery levy and therefore, in many cases because of the lack of this augmentation, salmon stocks have been allowed to decline accordingly. Surely this must be the most glaring case of 'cutting off your nose to spite your face' that anyone can possibly recall!

The present legislation passing through the House of Commons at the moment does definitely tighten up the poaching aspect by changing the onus of proof and bringing in dealer licences, both of which are steps in the right direction. However, there is no doubt that a tagging scheme would have been a far more efficient method of dealing with the marketing of salmon catches, and this in itself would have been strengthened if it had been backed up by a dealer licencing scheme, whereas a dealer licencing scheme itself will be far more difficult to enforce and far less effective in stamping out the dealing of poached fish on its own.

This legislation also provides a degree of flexibility in open and close seasons, weekend slack times and some aspects of schedule G concerning fish passes and smolts screening. It also defines and clears up many grey areas concerning district Boards, and widens the representation of people eligible to sit upon these boards by allowing not only proprietors of rod and net fishings but also anglers and netsmen to be represented. It also allows the chairman to be elected by the members of the Board instead of being automatically the owner of the highest rateable valued fishery in the district as he is now.

The Scottish Secretary, on application by a District Fishery Board, may make regulations restricting the use of certain baits and lures during certain times of the year and in certain areas of the district.

Certain vital aspects have been competely disregarded, though, in this new legislation. These are matters of finance, consultation on land development on the river's catchment, and any constructive banning or phasing out of the north-east coast of England Drift Net Fishery. All of which are matters of the utmost importance to the industry, and without any degree of control over these aspects it is difficult to see how District Salmon Fishery Boards can possibly carry out the remit with which they are charged efficiently. Salmon stocks will therefore be placed under greater pressure than they should be as a result of failure by the government once again to fully realise the importance of this resource.

UDN DISEASE

This destructive disease first appeared in salmon stocks in Ireland in 1965 and quickly spread through the salmon rivers of that country. In late 1966 it appeared in English rivers such as the Lune and Eden, then crossed to the Tweed on the east coast, spreading rapidly north and south on both coastlines, affecting most rivers in the country by 1969.

Although many of the world's leading virologists and bacteriologists strived to find out and isolate the type of bacteria or virus responsible, they have completely failed. They therefore gave this disease a descriptive name, namely Ulcerated Dermal Necrosis – UDN for short. It is interesting to note that a similar disease struck salmon stocks in Ireland in the late 1850s and followed a similar path to the outbreak in the 1960s. In those days a royal commission was set up to look into this threat to salmon stocks in the late 1850s. A bacteriologist, Mr Patterson, famed in the field at that time also failed to isolate the bacteria, and for this reason he also gave this disease a very apt name, namely *Bacillus Pestis.*

In both cases for the first few years mortality was extremely high in most affected rivers, but there is no doubt some rivers were more affected than others and strangely enough some rivers were worse affected in the spring, whilst others showed no signs of outbreaks in cold water temperatures and were only affected when the temperature of the water rose above 60°F during the summer. There is very little doubt from reading the evidence of the outbreak in the last century and from seeing photographs taken in that era, that UDN and *Bacillus Pestis* are one and the same disease.

We do not have accurate records to show the actual duration of the first outbreak but there is little doubt that it was present in salmon stocks in the Tweed from the late 1850s to sometime during the First World War, after which salmon stocks then remained unaffected until the 1967 outbreak.

In the initial stages this disease shows small open ulcers on the gill casing and head of the fish, and then a short time after the fish has entered fresh water these ulcers spread to the fin and body, followed by a white fungal growth which immerses not only the ulcers but a large part of the head, body and fins, often blinding the fish before it eventually dies. Because of the fact that this disease only became rampant in fresh water, net catches were hardly affected throughout the duration of the disease, but angling catches suffered extremely heavily. As the fish died there were fewer fish in the river to catch, but more importantly any fish, no matter how lightly affected, became completely lethargic and for this reason almost uncatchable.

At the time of writing this book nearly twenty years after the outbreak in 1967, salmon stocks in this country are still being affected. Although significant mortality in the stocks no longer occurs, marked fish are generally seen during some periods of the year. Probably 1985 was one of the worst years we have seen for the disease since the original outbreak, with many marked fish present in river systems over a long period of the season, but few mortalities. This badly affected angling catches on the worst affected rivers.

There is no doubt that in the early years of this recent outbreak angling catches suffered by almost 50% in the worst affected rivers, and even today when the disease is prevalent in the river systems this disease must affect the catch by at least 15% of the annual catch. In one case concerning the Welsh Dee in the late 1960s, shortly after the outbreak, mortality figures were so high that anglers were asked to stop fishing for the duration of the rest of the season, after the month of May. It is also interesting to note that in optimum angling heights of water, catches on the whole showed no marked decline, but as soon as the river became the slightest bit below optimum levels fish were almost impossible to catch, and this pattern still prevails even when the disease is hardly perceptible in the river.

Sea trout stocks also declined drastically as a result of this disease and are only just beginning to recover significantly in most areas of the country at the moment. Probably the main reason why they were so badly affected is the fact that sea trout, unlike salmon, return to fresh water to spawn year after year during their life. For example, a sea trout weighing sixteen pounds which I caught in the Kyle of Sutherland, had spawned no less than thirteen times according to the scale reading of this fish.

Any reduction of sea trout stocks from death by disease resulted in fewer surviving to return the following year, and in consequence less eggs available to incubate and regenerate the stocks for the future.

What no-one is in a position to assess is the actual damage that disease caused to the reproduction of salmon stocks during the early years after the outbreak in 1967, and how much bearing UDN disease really has had on the overall decline of salmon stocks, not only during that period, but up to the present time. We do know, however, in the initial years of the disease that there was a heavy mortality to salmon stocks prior to the spawning period and also that many heavily diseased fish were to be seen at spawning time. Whether these fish survived to complete the act of spawning is not known, but there is absolutely no doubt that spawning stocks were drastically reduced in our rivers between 1967 and 1975. We also know that some feeding parr in the river system died as a result of this disease, but whether these numbers were significant it is difficult to know for certain.

It may well be fact that a degree of immunity to the disease is passed on through the egg laid by diseased fish or built up in fry and parr which were present in the river system during the height of the disorder, but we cannot be sure whether the repercussions to these fish will show when they migrate to sea. We know that a fish entering fresh water during the height of the disease outbreak often became affected very quickly, but what we do not know is what happened to our young stock which had been in contact with the disease in fresh water when they migrated to the sea. Did they contract the disease? Unlikely, perhaps, but can we be sure?

Quite apart from the problems that I have listed above it is equally important that in the larger river systems that can accommodate several runs of fish these runs are kept in balance, so that there is no fear of one of these runs gaining predominance to the detriment of the others. As I have already explained, the winter and spring runs normally spawn in the highest areas of the catchment, the summer runs spawn in the middle reaches and their tributaries, and the autumn runs spawn in the lower reaches and their tributaries. The grilse that enter the river from mid-summer until the autumn can be the offspring of any of these runs of fish and normally spread themselves to the proximity of the nursery areas in the river on which they fed as fry and parr.

Naturally it is in the interest of every river system to accommodate as many runs as possible, in order that the river is productive for both rod and net enterprises for as long a duration of the season as possible. This not only creates a strong rod and net fishery on the river but also allows part of the revenue from these fisheries to be ploughed back as a fishery levy, and it can then be used to protect and improve the fishery in the particular river.

Winter run fish are available to be fished by anglers from the opening day of the season until the close of the rod fishery. Spring fish are also available to anglers for nine-tenths of the season, as well as being exploited by the net fishery over the duration of this run. Summer fish are available for angling for half of the season and can be exploited by net for the entire duration of the run and the same applies to summer running grilse. However, the autumn run has only just begun when the net season closes and this run, and the grilse component of it, are barely exploited by net or rod in the case of rivers that close to anglers on the 30th September. Even on rivers where angling closes in October or November, exploitation is by rod only for a maximum of eight weeks and in most cases two to four weeks.

The problem we are faced with today in Scotland is that runs of salmon are tending to get later and in the case of the autumn run, so lightly exploited at present, this run is naturally getting stronger and stronger and threatens at the moment to gain predominance over the other runs to the detriment of the salmon fishing industry on these river systems.

Unless something is done quickly to cull this particular run of fish to reasonable proportions, a large part of the spawning and feeding potential of river systems will become saturated by these fish which are hardly exploited by rod or net. They, therefore, contribute little to either the protection or conservation of salmon stocks in that river.

It is extraordinary that in a recent case where a District Board petitioned the Secretary of State to extend the net fishing season on the Deveron for a further fourteen days. The Secretary of State set up a Court of Enquiry which was adjudicated over by the Superintendant of Salmon Fisheries for Scotland. Having heard evidence from the DAFS's Salmon Fisheries Research Department scientists and other practical experts, who had spent their lifetime in this field and who favoured the extension, and other experts and many anglers supported by the Salmon Trout Association, who were against the extension, the Superintendent duly submitted his verdict to the Secretary of State advising him that the extension should be granted. The Secretary of State, however, overruled this decision and refused to grant the extension. Probably this is the greatest body blow that has ever been dealt out to the conservation of salmon stocks in Scotland. I have not the slightest doubt that the angling fraternity will, in the long run, realise their folly and rue the day they ever opposed this extension.

All these factors that I have listed and explained above are capable of having a significant bearing on the reduction of salmon stocks on their own account. But when combined together, acting at the same time, pressures on salmon stocks come close to breaking point. Over the past thirty years the salmon species has proved, beyond doubt, that it has tremendous resilience or by now it would have bowed out to these pressures and become virtually extinct in many of our river systems.

This resilience, strange to say, may have contributed partly to many of the problems that face the species at the present time. Central government has been loathe to act sooner on updating old legislation, and also to ban or run down the north-east coast drift net fishery, because catch statistics over this period have shown no drastic decline. What they fail to realise is that these statistics do not necessarily have any bearing on actual salmon stocks, nor the effort that is being used to produce these catches. It is the spawning stock, and they alone, that produce the smolts that migrate to sea.

The Nature Conservancy Council and other conservationists demand that we allow a quite unrealistic population of worthless mammals and cormorants to frequent our coastline, in spite of the fact that even if some of these colonies were reduced by five hundred times there would be no danger to those species, and disregard completely the pressure that these predators exert on such a valuable resource as salmon.

There is also no doubt that agriculture, forestry, and salmon fishery industries will always form the backbone of rural economy in Scotland. At the present time the former two receive subsidies and/or grant aid, as well as preferential de-rating or tax concessions, while the salmon industry is the poor relation and receives no public funding or any concessions. Nor does this industry even have the right of consultation or negotation regarding land developments that can, and often do, materially effect salmon stocks.

It is high time that everyone concerned got round a table in order that a plan can be drawn up to ease these problems. They will not go away, so they must be faced up to because if they are allowed to get any worse they will, in the end, eventually swamp the resilience of the species to the point of extinction.

Since this script was completed in the summer of 1986 no mention is made of the Salmon Advisory Committee set up by the Government recently. This Committee is to advise on the present state of salmon stocks in England, Wales and Scotland and also highlight other problems threatening the species. There is no doubt that the work of this Committee will produce valuable information on the subject.